ISLAM

Building Bridges
Of Understanding

A Jamaican Voice of Unity

IMAM DOUGLAS OWEN-ALI

LMH Publishing Limited

© 2004 Imam Douglas Owen-Ali
First Edition
10 9 8 7 6 5 4 3 2 1

'The book contains some seventy percent of the earlier book. *Islamic Law and International Relations*, 1998 - New Mind Productions.

Edited by Julia Tan/Mike Henry/Charles Moore

Cover Design by Lee-Quee Design

Book Design & Layout by Michelle M.A. Mitchell, PAGE Services

Published by LMH Publishing Limited
7 Norman Road,
LOJ Industrial Complex
Building 10
Kingston C.S.O., Jamaica
Tel: 876-938-0005; 938-0712
Fax: 876-759-8752
Email: lmhbookpublishing@cwjamaica.com
Website: www.lmhpublishingjamaica.com

Printed in the U.S.A.   ISBN 976-8184-58-2

Dedication

This book is dedicated to my role model, teacher and mentor an outstanding Jamaican Patriot and Statesman, my beloved father, of blessed memory Eric 'Milo Rock' Owen.

To: My beloved mother, Mrs. Pauline Owen, for enduring the trial of motherhood. Let us revere the womb that bore us. Give thanks to the Almighty Creator, for all our mothers around the world.

To: My Project Coordinator Helena Williams. My profound thanks and sincere gratitude for her patience and tolerance in making this project a reality. Let's get ready to roll! We must give thanks to the Almighty Creator for His blessings.

To: A beloved brother, teacher and patriot, the late Stokely Carmichael (Kwame Toure'). We will always be "Ready for a revolution", (peace be unto you). The struggle continues.

To: Ambassador The Honorable Keith Johnson O.J.; C.D.; (Uncle Keith), A Quintessential Diplomat, patriot, statesman, father, teacher, mentor and mend. Uncle Keith you are a living legend. Special thanks and much love.

To: A true Jamaican Legend, statesman, scholar, teacher and patriot the late Honorable Glenville Owen, O.D., a legacy that remains timeless.

To: My Uncle the late Stafford Owen, one of the most positive thinkers of all time.

To: My beloved sister Cecile Owen-Campbell and her husband Michael, my special nephew Warren and my special niece Melissa. Thanks for your love and support and for being a very special part of this journey of faith.

To: My Aunt Angela Gray a special thank you.

To: Ruby Martin and Marsha Nesbeth and my beloved family at the Maxfield Park Children's home. I will always be "a friend of the unbefriended poor". Much love always.

To: My beloved friend Margaret Rose McNeil. Much love.

To: Special thanks to my friend and distinguished photographer Howard Lewis, it will always be "The Utmost For The Highest."

To: Dr. Ruth Doorbar, providing unwavering inspiration. Never give up!

To: Dr. William (Billy) Lockyer, thanks for your unconditional love and friendship.

To: Ted Emanuel for inspiring me with the knowledge and consciousness of the precious gift of health and life.

To: Barbara Ifill-Bennett for keeping me healthy and for her patience, love and support.

To: Beloved Minister Andrew Muhammad and beloved Minister Clive Muhammad and the Nation of Islam family in Jamaica. Thanks for your love and support. The journey of faith continues.

To: My beloved spiritual teacher, mentor, brother and friend, Sheikh Ahmed Tijani of the Universal Center of America for his love, spiritual guidance and divine understanding. We give thanks for affording me the opportunity to be of service to Islam and to humanity.

To: The Executive members of the Global Oneness Family. Delroy Webster (Mustafa) (president), Archibald Hammond (Jabir) (Executive Vice President). Your friendship, love and support in this journey of faith have been invaluable. Howard Malcolm, (Legal Counsel); for being a brother and true friend. Melvin Seid, (Chief of Security); for your unconditional love. Moneyede Martin; (Director of Marketing and Road Manager), Your friendship, support, generosity and brotherly love make you a rare gem. May Almighty Allah bless our efforts.

iv

To: Colin Leslie, my esteemed Cultural Advisor for his guidance and inspiration and for keeping the mission real. Much respect.

To: Beloved Brother Kwame, (Chief Security Officier) for your dedication and loyalty.

To: Tia Farquharson, (Entertainment Coordinator) for your generous support.

To: Ransford White, for his support and generosity in keeping the mission alive.

To: Christopher Issa, for keeping the dream alive.

To: Her Excellency Ambassador Sue Cobb, Mr. Richard Smyth, (Deputy Chief of Mission), Mr. Donald Wells, (Consul General), Orna Blum, (Public Affairs Officer), Emma Lewis, Public Affairs Associate Angella Harvey, (Senior Cultural Exchanges Coodinator, Office of Public Affairs) Myrna Lewis, (Information Resource Center Director), Natalie Rose, (Office of Public Affairs), Nicole Hylton (Consul General's Office), Olive Creary (Consul General's Office), Barbara DeLeon (Office of the Ambassador), Jeannie S. Keller (Office of the Ambassador) and the entire United States Embassy Community in Jamaica, I offer my profound thanks and gratitude for the support and bond of friendship. May freedom and liberty continue to ring for humanity across the earth. Let us continue the global mission of building bridges of understanding, humanity and hope for the human family.

To: To my dear friends at the British High Commission in Kingston, Jamaica, Deputy High Commissioner Mr. Phil Sinkinson and Mr. Tony Ridout, First Secretary Chancery and Rowena Conner, I offer my special thanks and sincere gratitude for your moral support in the mission of building bridges of understanding around the world.

To: My father, brother, mentor and teacher, The Distinguished Leader of the Nation of Islam The Honorable Minister Louis Farrakhan, you are a priceless gift from Almighty Allah (God) to humanity.

To: Leonard Farrakhan Muhammad, (Chief of Staff) Nation of Islam, much thanks in keeping the mission alive.

To: Richard Muhammad, (Editor, Final Call Newspaper), the message is one love, one heart, one humanity.

To: Mustafa and Joshua Farrakhan, for the bond of friendship and brotherly love.

To: The Nation of Islam Family around the Globe, may the dream of freedom, peace, justice, and equality rein for the entire brotherhood of man and sisterhood of woman. As Salaam Alaikum. (peace be Unto You).

To: My esteemed Publisher Mike Henry, for turning the vision into reality. Much thanks.

To: Dawn Chambers, Julia Tan and the LMH Publishing family for turning dreams into reality. We give thanks to the Creator for success in this endeavor.

To: Dr. Oswald Harding, C.D., Q.C., a great teacher, father and friend. Thank you.

To: Howard Hamilton, Q.C., for your support and encouragement in this global mission.

To: Shiah Coore and his distinguished team, for creating the accompaniment for the song, *Building Bridges.* Much thanks.

To: Ron Muschette for inspiring great music and a divine message.

To: Rudy Valentino for giving us great music.

To: Heather Cummings and Rashida Rose for giving the music life.

To: Joy Cole for her friendship.

To: Arthan Coleman for his spiritual guidance and for believing in me.

To: Brother Mustafa Abdul-Hakim Dyer for being a true friend and brother.

To: Brother Stephen Henriques, Ainslsey Henriques and all the members of the Jewish community in Jamaica for their kind cooperation and the spirit of mutual acceptance, friendship and brotherhood.

To: Lavern Dawes you are a rare gem of love, inspiration and friendship.

To: Brother Ronald Waite for the precious gift of friendship.

To: Keith Summers, a special thank you for your support.

To: Phillip Lodge, for being a special part of this journey of faith.

To: The entire Global Oneness Family I offer a special thank you for your love, support and patience in this journey of faith.

To: To Brother Errol Hanchard, and Brother Paul Burke and to Jamomes Developers Ltd., I offer my sincere thanks for your material and moral support. Let us continue to *build bridges of understanding.*

To: Michelle M.A. Mitchell, typesetter, for giving us a great product.

To: All those special persons who have supported me in this incredible journey of faith, (Iman) words cannot express my profound thanks and sincere gratitude in the realization of this universal mission and the goal of Building Bridges of Understanding, Humanity and Hope for the human family. "Justice for every race, equality in every place. Freedom from economic depression". May Almighty Allah richly bless you all.

To: All those persons whom I may have failed to mention in this dedication, I offer my sincere thanks and gratitude to you all.

Finally, and most importantly, all praise is due to the Creator Almighty Allah, (God) for giving me the precious gift of life, and for preserving me, and inspiring me with faith (Iman) and for his mercy, compassion and rich blessings. **Allah is the greatest! Allah is the greatest! Allah is the greatest! As Salaam Alaikum (peace be unto you).**

Publisher's Statement

NEW DESCRIPTION OF
BUILDLNG BRIDGES OF UNDERSTANDING.

The week of September 11, 2001, presently culminating in the Islamic war, has brought the western world of plenty face to face with the need to understand the depth of the wounds and scars of the worlds' suffering poor as well as their deep-seated anger.

Religion like politics, forms the core element of all that we yearn for, and the world, especially the Western World needs to understand, in simple but profound terms, that the teaching of any religion and the belief in one's religion and country, is as deep and wide as the chasm that divides east and west, and north and south.

That the three great religions Christianity, Judaism and Islam had their beginnings in the same city, Jerusalem, is sometimes a forgotten fact.

Many books have been written about the subject of Islam, but it is our feeling that a simple text, which introduces the layman to Islam and its wider impact on man's thoughts and on its followers, will only help to separate the passion of misunderstanding, from the pain of misdirected deeds.

'The book' contains some seventy percent of the earlier book (*Islamic Law and International Relations*, 1998 - New Mind Productions.) and we hope that its intent, to separate the extremist from the 'purest', will be achieved by its updated message, written by a converted Jamaican to Islam, and one who sees the need to broaden the spectrum of International Relations.

For indeed, the recent happenings reflect the need for a new world order and new world thinking.

MIKE HENRY, CD, MP
Publisher.

Contents

Foreword

The publication of this revised edition, aptly titled *Islam - Building Bridges of Understanding. A Jamaican Voice of Unity*, by Imam Douglas Owen - Ali at this juncture in contemporary world history, is very timely and makes eminent sense. The infamous and tragic events of Tuesday, September 11th, 2001, which saw the demonstration of religious extremists disguised as Islamic fundamentalism implicated in the killing of thousands of innocent persons on the mainland of the world's sole surviving superpower, the USA, and the subsequent bombing of Afghanistan, has left millions around the world to question not only their own mortality but more urgently to apply intelligent thought to cultural examination of conscience in the quest for lasting world peace.

This is a very readable and human book that seeks to place both the purity and compassion of the religion of Islam, Islamic Law and Jurisprudence among the constellation of world ideas and thought, seeking to build a world with more partners and no room for terrorists. It eschews fanaticism and insanity in the approach to solving the myriad of complex problems facing the world. For despite the advances of science and technology, the future of humankind is still very uncertain, and without a doubt, poverty, wars, hopelessness and human misery can only be overcome by intelligent thought and action, rather than by bombs and acts of terrorism. Ultimately, as the author reminds us, the world's future is guaranteed in the application, to problems and challenges, of moderation, balanced pragmatism and old fashion good sense.

This book reflects both the author's rich and extensive experience as a practicing and devout Muslim and his tremendous courage and selflessness at time when Islam as a legitimate world religion is the target of much international misunderstanding and hostility.

Imam Douglas Owen-Ali is that rare combination of an individual who combines scholarship and a deep interest in research, with qualities of dedication, strong commitment to his religion and the quest for universal justice and a genuine and lasting world peace. Above all, he is a true humanitarian, sensitive to personal concerns, and deeply moved by human needs in the field of international politics and economic relations. This has led him to work tirelessly in an unending cycle of teaching, research, intellectual and spiritual leadership as the International Ambassador of Peace representing the Universal Islamic Center of America, based in Chicago Illinois, with responsibility for Jamaica and the wider Caribbean region.

Despite the tragic events of what has come to be known as 9/11 (the 9th of September, 2001) humankind's passion for freedom, justice and personhood remains as fierce as ever. Against this background, the author understands the need for unmitigated fervor in the struggle for Rights and Justice around the globe, even in the face of failure, to rid the world of the persistent obscenities of political, economic, social ethnic and religious conflicts that have plagued the majority of humanity for the past half a millennium.

I warmly congratulate the author on producing a digestible, relevant and non-technical book. I expect that it will enjoy substantial circulation in the Caribbean region and beyond. It deserves no less.

MR. HOWARD HAMILTON,
Q.C., Public Defender for Jamaica
Office of Public Defender
78 Harbour Street
Kingston, Jamaica
December 19, 2001

Introduction

The author, Imam Douglas Owen-Ali, seeks to bring a message of economic and spiritual empowerment to those whom he encounters, by broadening their exposure to Islam's cultural ways and beliefs, to enlarge their respect for Islam, and to cultivate in them the fear of Allah (Taqwah).

The style of his text is very autobiographical in which the author sometimes reveals his innermost feelings and thoughts. The philosophy is simple, bordering on naivete; this is part of its charm and seduction. He calls for a divine world order and world peace, recognizing that this is not achievable without universal justice. He knows that peace is hard process but a process that will ultimately save humanity. Owen-Ali has begun a journey of faith and has chosen Islam as his spiritual path, for to him the fundamental principles of Islam are about peace and compassion for all and with enlightened tolerance.

Owen-Ali's task of bringing his message has become more challenging since September 11 and the exposure of the Islamic Taliban Regime in Afghanistan and the international recognition of the Muslim based Al Qaeda and its link to terrorism. How can he now convey his message of the virtues of Islam at a time when, in a great part of the Western World, international terrorism is viewed as the step-child of Islam? How can he succeed in building bridges of Understanding, Humanity and Hope in a climate of hostility and recriminations as is evidenced in the Israeli - Palestinian conflict to which he alludes in his thoughts on the Middle-East crisis?

As a Muslim convert, the author's task is to interpret Islam's spiritual message to the Western World. In the words of Paul Bruton, whom he quotes:

"It is a matter of great regret that so little is known of the Islamic faith by the average Westerner, even that little is usually partly erroneous, if not wholly incorrect."[1]

Before Owen-Ali's message can fall on fertile ground or receive a listening ear, he must confront the perception of the Shariah Law and the understanding of *Jihad* in the minds of his targeted audience.

Jihad is perhaps one of the most misunderstood of all aspects of Islam in the West.[2] It is taken to mean military engagement or holy war; yet the word *Jihad*, as explained to me, means striving or struggle, and in a spiritual sense is a constant battle against sin in all its aspects. It is, for Muslims, striving to be pure and to resist evil.

In the West, Shariah has also aroused the greatest misgivings and most intense hostility.[3] The recently ordered stoning of a Nigerian woman under Shariah Law, for having a child out of wedlock, drew world wide condemnation.

I am told that 'Shariah' means the path to be followed, the way of Islam and the general title of Islamic Law:

*Show us the straight way. The way of those who
(portion) is not wrath, and who do not go astray.
Qur'an-Surah 1:6-7.*

The Shariah is a detailed code of conduct or the cannon comprising ways and modes of worship, standard of morals and life, laws that allow and prescribe and judge between right and wrong. Unlike the *Din*, which is the faith of Islam and which undergoes no change whatsoever, we are told that matters of the Shariah are frequently amended according to the needs of the time and society.[4] This is a clear necessity, for the modern demands and pressures in a technological age require a reassessment or refinement of legal principles that were laid down fourteen centuries ago. Muslims employ modern reason and judgement to decide the course of action that is in greatest accordance with the spirit of the Qur'an and *hadith* (sayings) of the Prophet. This working out of Muslim principles in the modern age is called *ijtihad*; and where actions which have to be decided have no clear guidance, they are decided by conscience, *mubah*.

Imam Douglas-Ali has to convince his audience that many of the unacceptable practices regarded as 'Islamic' are not in the least Islamic, but are the actions and culture in keeping with the spirit of the Qur'an and *hadith* (sayings) of the prophet. This working out of Muslim principles in the modern age is called *ijtihad;* and where actions which have to be decided have no clear guidance, they are decided by conscience, *mubah*.

Imam Douglas-Ali has to convince his audience that many of the unacceptable practices regarded as 'Islamic' are not in the least Islamic, but are the actions and culture of rulers and governments that may well govern Islamic people but are at variance with the laws of Islam. The laws of Islam, when properly interpreted and carried out are always merciful and not barbaric.[5]

Imam Owen-Ali calls for a balanced and moderate approach in solving both national and international affairs.[6] The tyrannical zeal for an extremist form of Islam is not *Sunnah*. *(Trespassing beyond the truth) Surah* 5:77

> "*O people of The Book! Do not exceed in your religion, the bounds (of what is proper)*"
> "*O believers, do not make unlawful those good things which Allah has made lawful for your, and commit no excess. God* loves *not those given to excess.*
>
> Surah 5:87

As a student of international relations, in the text, the author averts to The Middle-East crisis, the new era of co-operation between the United States and Russia, the India and Pakistan conflict and the United States and Cuba relations. He will now have to turn his thoughts to the war with Iraq - a Muslim country – and ask himself what role will Turkey, another Muslim state, play in such a possible conflict. In fact, what role will

Muslim nations of the Middle East play in any new international conflict, bearing in mind his aim of the attainment of Islamic ideas in international affairs and global policy making. What thoughts has he towards the "axis of evil" (declared by the United States, the country of his citizenship; of which he proudly declares)? Now is the test of his faith: how does he engage the thinking of the world with the teachings of the *Holy Qur'an* and the *Sunnah?* The task that he faces is a formidable one, if not daunting.

But he claims a reputation of not backing away from challenges.[7] His declared mission is to serve humanity. He demonstrated this aspect of his character when The Honourable Minister Louis Farrakhan, the controversial leader of The Nation of Islam, who some in the United States had labeled 'anti-semitic, visited the island of Jamaica in March 2002: when, through Owen Ali's instrumentality, Farrakhan joined in the Saturday morning worship at the Jewish Synagogue in Kingston, where gifts were exchanged and new friendship forged. Perhaps on that occasion, the author felt as though he was "Bilal, (the Negro Slave who was the first Caller to prayer) *(Muezzin)*. It was Bilal who, after the 'final sermon' of the prophet (pbuh) at Mount Arafat, could be heard calling the people to prayer.

Convinced that: the humanism in Islamic Law and Jurisprudence will bring about a fairer world; technological development alone will not solve the human problems of war, poverty and human misery; Islam is a religion of peace and universal brotherhood; and entrusted as an international ambassador of peace, representing the universal Islamic Center of America, with a mission of building bridges of humanity and hope for the human family, and developing mutual acceptance amongst persons of different religions, political, economic and social persuasion; like Bilal, he now calls the people to prayer; to join him in this endeavour. Will this intrepid proselytizer accomplish this? *Inshallah* - If *Allah* wills it.

Dr. O.G. Harding, O.J., C.D., Q.C., Ph.D.
Research Fellow - U.W.I.

Chapter One

The Nature and Scope of Islamic Law and Jurisprudence

1.1   INTRODUCTION

It is most appropriate to begin this discussion by first stating the "Five Pillars of Islam". It is only when one understands these five pillars of the Islamic religion that a positive and unbiased approach will be given to the relevance of Islamic law and Jurisprudence in present day international relations and diplomacy.

1. **The Creed:** Proclaiming the unity of God with the declaration "There is no God but Allah". Muhammad is the messenger of God. This declaration of faith in Almighty Allah is called *SHAHADA*. This is the first foundation of faith in the religion of Islam.

2. **Prayer:** Performed five times each day, facing the Qiblah. Prayer in Islam is called *SALAAT*. This is the second foundation.

3. **Fasting:** Abstinence from food, liquid and sexual intercourse from dawn to sunset during the holy month of Ramadan. This third foundation is referred to as *SAWM*.

4. **Charity:** The fourth foundation in Islam is the wealth tax which is *ZAKAAT*. This is the payment of a certain percentage of one's wealth for distribution to the poor.

5. **Pilgrimage to the House** *(HAJJ)* This is the fifth foundation in Islam. This involves the performance of a pilgrimage to the House in Makkah, at least once in a person's life, provided means for the journey are available.

These five pillars in the religion of Al-Islam form the corner-stone of every aspect of Islamic pursuit. "Man has learned how to walk on the moon but he has not yet learned how to live on earth". Man has made enormous strides in technological advancement, but remains void in his spiritual, moral and social duties. Human beings have not yet learnt how to behave and interact with one another. It is my sincere hope that this work will be read by Muslims and non-Muslims. As sons and daughters of Adam and Eve, we are all brothers and sisters. We all yearn for an improvement in the quality of our human relationships.

We are all fellow-passengers abroad spaceship Earth – need our inner worlds be so far apart? As mankind is now in the twenty-first century, it is with great hope that the ideals of peace, justice, equity and fair play will not remain mere ideals, but rather principles that will be practised and promoted not only amongst fellow human beings, but by policy makers in the international political and economic arena as well.

The super powers must now ardently strive to adopt foreign policy strategies that will bring equal justice to all mankind regardless of race, creed, color, ethnicity, geographical location, political or economic stature. It is only "Equal Rights and Justice" that will prevent continuous human conflict around the globe. Technological development by itself will not eradicate wars, poverty, hopelessness and human misery.

It is in light of this that this book proffers that Islamic Law and Jurisprudence are not only relevant in present day international relations and diplomacy, but offers practical and viable solutions in a world plagued by political, economic, social and ethnic conflicts. Islamic Law and Jurisprudence could correct the present injustices in international affairs, if given the opportunity, and also if it is applied with due care and moderation.

Let me state unequivocally that this book does not call for a "fanatic" or insane approach in solving the complex and enormous problems that plague our world today. Rather, it calls for a moderate and balanced approach in solving both national and international conflicts with the ultimate aim being the security of mankind. For this security to become a reality, however, "Divine Justice" must be attainable on earth. There can and will be no peace if Divine Justice remains an elusive dream. This call for Divine Justice must not be seen as some idealistic utopia on earth but rather as a way forward if the sanctity of all mankind is to be preserved. It will ensure that all human beings will be given the opportunity to live on earth the way that Almighty God, Allah, intended it to be, not the way MAN has distorted it to suit his own selfish interests. The time has now come for world leaders and leaders of thought around the globe to look objectively and purposefully at the future of all mankind, if indeed mankind has a future!

By no means does this work suggest that Islamic Law and Jurisprudence will offer a panacea for all human and global conflicts. What in fact Islamic Law and Jurisprudence offers is a more humanistic approach in solving the plagues of injustice, armed conflicts, socio-economic disparities and perpetual human misery. This humanism in Islamic Law and Jurisprudence will indeed bring about a "fairer" world whereby equity, justice, morality, peace and equal rights will become not only attainable ideals, but possibly a way of life in both national and international affairs. I quote the famous writer and philosopher, George Bernard Shaw, who said: "Some people see things and say why, while others see things and say why not". It will be appropriate to look briefly at the Prophet Muhammad (may the peace and blessing of Allah forever be upon him).

Muhammad, the great prophet was born at Makkah in the ruling and aristocratic clan of the Quraysh, a branch of the Islamilite family. As a boy, Muhammad did not have the opportunity of getting a formal scholastic education. He remained an unlettered man but he was an embodiment of all virtues. Sweet and amiable in his nature and honest, trustworthy and truthful in all his dealings, he won the love and respect of the Quraysh and was called "Al Ameen", or "The Trustworthy". The Makkans had great admiration for his wisdom, intelligence and uprightness. In critical moments, they would succumb to his judgement and would gladly accept his decision. Muhammad was the perfect politician, diplomat, spiritual guide and, most of all, the perfect human being.

Muhammad became a prophet at the age of forty after receiving Divine Revelation from Almighty God, Allah. Allah favoured him with divine guidance and with a mission to set an ideal religion and an ideal society in the world. After this first revelation, the verses of the Qur'an were revealed to Prophet Muhammad during the twenty-two years of his prophetic career. The Qur'an remained the embodiment of Divine Guidance to Muhammad as he embarked on his new mission. This new mission of the Holy Prophet Muhammad (may the peace and blessings of Allah be upon him) was called Islam. Islam is the religion of peace and universal brotherhood. It is a belief in Divine Monotheism, that is, belief in one Supreme Divine Being, Allah. It protests against idolatry, inequality, injustice and all the evil ways of man and society. Islam enjoins its followers to lead a pure, simple and decent life. The believers of the Islamic faith are called Muslims.

George Bernard Shaw noted that: "Islam is the only religion which appears to me to possess the assimilating capabilities to the changing phase of existence, which can make it appeal to every age. I believe that if a man like Muhammad were to assume dictatorship of the modern world, he would succeed in solving its problems in a way that would bring it much needed peace and happiness. If any religion has the chance of ruling over England, nay Europe, within the next one hundred years, it can only be Islam. The wonderful vitality of Islam makes it supreme in all facets of human interaction and endeavor".

The writer Paul Brunton too, saw the beneficial effects of Islam. "It is a matter of great regret that so little is known of the Islamic faith by the average Westerner; even that little is usually partly erroneous, if not wholly incorrect. Muhammad taught men not to be ashamed to kneel and worship the Invisible King, to go down on their knees in the open streets". This book has

4

taken the liberty to deviate from the topic, so as to create valuable insight to the religion of Islam and the Holy Prophet Muhammad (may the peace and blessings of Allah forever be upon him). For it is only when we can truly understand and appreciate the religion of Islam and its tenets that we are able to see the practicability and relevance of Islamic Law and Jurisprudence in present day international relations and diplomacy. Islamic law must no longer be perceived as some "fanatic ideal" in international affairs and diplomatic relations.

1.2   The Nature and Scope of Islamic Law and Jurisprudence

Islamic law and jurisprudence is a comprehensive system that offers solutions to local, national and international problems. The onus, however, is on the scholars in Islam to adapt Islamic law and jurisprudence to fit the present international system. By adapt, we mean adjusting the Islamic principles to accommodate present day realities in international political and economic matters. However, let me categorically state that adapt does not mean to compromise the core principles and tenets of the religion of Islam of Islamic law and jurisprudence, but rather to apply moderation, balance, pragmatism and good sense in matters concerning national and international problems. Islamic law and jurisprudence covers all facets of human and worldly endeavor. It is, therefore, dynamic and not static. It does not operate in isolation from man's secular needs, or his physical and material aspirations. It works in conjunction with them. Justice is Allah's attribute, and to stand firm for justice is to be a witness to Allah, even if it is detrimental to our interests as we conceive them or the interests of those who are near and dear to us. According to the Latin saying, "Let justice be done though heaven should fall". But Islamic justice is higher than the formal justice of Roman law or any other human law. It is even more penetrative than the subtler justice in the specu-

5

lation of the Greek philosophers. It searches out the innermost motives, because we are to act as in the presence of Almighty Allah to whom all things, acts and motives are known. The nature and scope of Islamic law and jurisprudence has no limits. It offers solutions and viable alternatives to every aspect of life on earth. This is so because its injunctions are Divine. It seeks to make justice the cornerstone of its nature and its scope. This Divine justice remains the philosophical guideline in every sphere of human activity, be it spiritual, material, social, political and financial.

What is Shariah?

To understand the essence of the *Shariah* one must first understand the relationship between man and God that Islam proposes. There is no God but one God; Muhammad is the Prophet and messenger of God: this simple sentence is the bedrock of the Islamic Creed. God is the creator; to Him alone therefore belongs the kingdom and He is the only Sovereign:

"Surely your Lord is God who has created the heavens and the earth...verily to Him belong the creation and the sovereignty" (al-Arra'f 7:54).

And:

"He has created the heavens and the earth with a purpose, He wraps night about day and He wraps day about night...He has created you from one being...That then is God, your only Lord; His is the Kingdom. There is no God but He." (al-Zumar 39:5-6)

God is the Creator. To Him alone therefore, as his only Lord and master, man must submit his entire being: *"Your God is one God, so only to Him submit"* (al-Hajj 22:34).

The essence of *Shariah* is to enable man on earth, who is Allah's representative on earth, to establish justice for everybody. It is also a deterrent which prevents crimes and maintains order in a civilized society. But, paradoxically, it is the *Shariah* which, more than any other element in Islam, seems to arouse the greatest misgivings and most intense of fears, hostility and ridicule both among those who are not within the fold of Islam and those Muslims who are either unaware of or have become spiritually and intellectually alienated from their own traditions. For many of them, the *Shariah* is something barbaric, cruel, inhuman and uncivilized, which is trying to turn the clock back on progress and modernization and plunge the world back into the Dark Ages (as if it was 'dark' in the world of Islam at the time it was 'dark' in Europe!). Women will be no better than slaves and non-Muslims treated as second class citizens. Cut off the hand of a thief, stone the adulterer, veil the woman; this, according to its opponents is the sum-substance of that *Shariah* which is so deeply inspiring Muslims everywhere in the world today. *Shariah* is an Arabic word meaning "the path to be followed". Literally, it means 'the way to a watering place'. It is the path not only leading to Allah the Most High, but the path believed by all Muslims to be the path shown by Allah, the Creator Himself, who taught His messenger Prophet Muhammad (peace be upon him). In Islam, Allah alone is the sovereign and it is He who has the right to ordain a path for the guidance of mankind. Thus, it is only *Shariah* that liberates man from *servitude* to other than Almighty Allah. This is the only reason why Muslims are obliged to strive for the implementation of that path, and that of no other path.

The *Shariah* originated from the direct commandments of Allah; but there is the provision of power given to man in order to interpret and expand Divine commandment, by means of analogical deductions and through other processes unlike the Roman law which developed from the action or English common law which developed from the writs. The very first source of *Shariah* is the *Holy Qur'an*. The second source is the *Sunnah* or the practice of Prophet Muhammad (S.A.W.) who has rightly explained: "I leave two things for you: you will never go astray

7

while holding them firmly–the Book of Allah and the Sunnah of his Prophet."

The third source is *Ijma* consensus of opinion. The *Shariah* thought process aims at regulating the relationship of man with Allah and man with man. This is the reason why the Shariah law cannot be separated from Islamic ethics.

The fourth source, the exercise of reason and judgement to determine the Shariah, is called *Ijtihad*. It subsumes various categories of endeavor such as opinion, analogy, public good and so on. It is a key element in ensuring the dynamism of the *Shariah*, but it is often misunderstood. The central notion of justice in the *Shariah* is based on mutual respect of one human being by another. The just society in Islam means the society that secures and maintains respect for persons through various social arrangements that are in the common interest of all its members. Respect for person in the *Shariah* is noted in Divine injunctions of the *Qur'an* and the precepts of the Prophet. The Bill of Rights, Suffrage, Civil Rights and the slogans for political and economic equality, as we know them today, are of a very recent origin and seem to be mere reflections of what the *Shariah* taught 1400 years ago from now. The treatment accorded by the *Shariah* made the aristocracies of birth, race, wealth, language the features which vary from person to person as suspect and disrespectful of persons. The criterion of respect was only *taqwah*–the fear of Allah. "The best among you in the eyes of Allah are those who are stronger in *taqwah* (fear of Allah)". The *Shariah*, it should be noted, gives priority to human welfare over human liberty. Muslims, as well as non-Muslims, living in a Muslim state are duty bound not to exploit common resources to their own advantage. Since a man in Islam is not merely an economic animal, each person has equal right to life and to a decent standard of living, and, thus, has priority over the so called "economic liberty".

Judicial power, according to *Shariah*, must always operate in conformity with equality, even to the benefit of an enemy and to detriment of a relative, *Shariah* does not allow the slightest

8

modification in the rule of "Perfect Justice", or any form of arbitrary procedure to replace it. It firmly establishes the rule of law, eliminating all differences between the high and low. The *Qur'an* asserts that all mankind, born of the same father and mother, form one single family and that the God of men is unique. The Creator has ordered men according to nations and tribes so that they may know and assist one another for the good of all, not to despise one another. The *Shariah* experiences no tension between "love and law" or between "faith and deeds". Both are integrated into a harmonious whole.

The *Shariah* is, for all times to come, equally valid under all circumstances. The *Shariah*, however, cannot be adulterated to suit the whims and fancies of human values and standard as it is divinely ordained. It is rather the absolute norm to which all human values and conduct must conform. It is the ultimate frame of reference for man; it is the scale on which man's action and conduct must be weighed. The basic principles of the *Shariah*, therefore, can be summed up as follows:-

(a) The larger interest of the society takes precedence over the interest of the individual.

(b) Although relieving hardship and promoting benefit are both among the prime objectives of the *Shariah*, the former takes precedence over the latter.

(c) A bigger loss cannot be inflicted to relieve a smaller loss or a bigger benefit cannot be sacrificed for a smaller one. Conversely, a smaller harm cannot be inflicted to avoid a bigger harm nor can a smaller benefit be sacrificed for a larger one.

It is with sincere hope that *Shariah* law will begin to play a vital role in future International Affairs and Diplomatic Relations. As our world remains constantly plagued by multifarious conflicts, it is only the practical application of "Divine Justice" as prescribed in *Shariah* that will ultimately alleviate and eradicate human misery on God's precious earth.

1.3   Islamic Law, Myth or Reality?

It is time that some of the grave misconceptions about Islam and Islamic law be addressed. Neither Islam nor Islamic law is a myth; nor are they alien. Islamic culture may appear alien, especially to the western mind, but it is surely not alien. Islamic culture is now a potent force both spiritually and morally around the four corners of the globe. International law makers can no longer wish that Islamic law will one day quickly disappear. It will not! Foreign policy strategists had better take note of the reality of Islamic Law and Jurisprudence. Islamic law is not some passing fad that comes and goes according to changing consumer fancies. It is from Almighty Allah, the creator of all creation. It is in the light of the present complexities in world affairs that this book proffers, once again, that Islamic law can be the salvation for all mankind. There can be no peace without justice and there can be no justice without the practical formulation of Islamic legal policies in the national and international arena. If Islamic law is perceived as a myth, then justice could also be seen as a myth.

For so long man has groped endlessly to translate faith and moral ideals into viable actions and deeds. Some have been tempted to separate the two and others have been led into a never-enduring philosophical quest. They have been able to define what is ethical, moral or good. Not that all ethical and moral problems have been solved and buried for ever. Not that Islamic law will immediately solve the enormous problems on the earth. So long as man is alive, he will continue to face hard and difficult choices and dilemmas, old and new. This is a natural corollary of a world view where man has to battle incessantly for "good" against "evil"! Islamic law offers new solutions and suggestions to the vast problems of man's inhumanity to man and to the present crisis in the international political and economic arena. Islamic law, therefore, has the means to find the best way to ease and facilitate this arduous task.

10

Chapter 2

The Understanding of Islamic Law and Jurisprudence

2.1   The Understanding of Islamic Law and Jurisprudence Vis-à-vis Present Day International Relations and Diplomacy

Islamic international law encompasses all public functions conducted by the state of its private citizens in any intercourse not necessarily subject to private regulations in the performance of the public needs and functions. Since we have discussed the characteristics of the *Shariah*, we should bear in mind that individual freedom is sacred within ethical limits imposed by the *Shariah*, and it will be considered only as long as it does not conflict with the larger social interests or as long as the individual does not transgress the rights of others.

The Prophet Muhammad (PBUH) was the greatest politician and he did not forget to respect the treaties and pledges, but he held on the contrary a great importance to the strict observance of the terms of treaties entered into by Muslims. Sometimes in observing the terms of treaties, he had to forego the advantage of his little Commonwealth of Islam which functioned on the principle of *Shariah*.

The main emphasis of the *Shariah* is on the sanctity of a legal due process concept to guarantee the life, liberty, property and honour of every human being. Therefore, Muslim law is the fair regulation of conduct for the faithful in this world and in the world hereafter. Islamic international law aims at the fair regulation of the Muslim state in its foreign relations. It is directed also to the individual Muslim state and non-Muslim states. Prophet Muhammad (may peace be upon him) was a great respecter of international law and was also the perfect embodiment of the ideal diplomat. It is in the light of this background, that it becomes much easier to understand the dynamism of Islamic Law and Jurisprudence, in present day International Relations and Diplomacy. It is, however, very unfortunate that many international law makers, diplomats and foreign policy strategies see Islamic and jurisprudence as an irrelevant factor in settling international disputes. The call for a new international economic order, was that not a call for economic and social justice? When the developing nations of the world call for a level playing field in international trade and economic participation, this is no doubt a call for "equal rights and justice". Is this not the essence of Islamic law? When the great superpower, the United States of America, initiated "Operation Desert Hope" in Somalia to restore hope for many of the dying people in that region, was not that in essence an Islamic duty? Yes it was! Recent events in South Africa are a vivid example. The conscience of the world community, regardless of race, creed or colour, was sensitized to the abhorrent system of racial injustice in South Africa known as "apartheid". This system of apartheid was a flagrant insult to the dignity of mankind. Dr. Nelson Mandela's rise to the Presidency of South Africa was an Islamic call for "Divine Justice". The International Reparations Crusade which calls for reparations to Africa and Africans in the Diaspora is an appeal for "human justice". There is a principle in law known as unjust enrichment: if one party becomes enriched as a result of a wrong done to another party, the law compels the former to make an adjustment of the latter. In the religion of Islam, it is one's piety, one's submission to Almighty Allah that gives one supremacy, not the colour of one's skin. It is in light of this that this book takes the position that Islamic law and jurisprudence has always been relevant in International Relations and Diplomacy. It is not some "new idea" whose time has come.

The fundamental principle of the Islamic legal system, is that the laws of Islam, are not passed in a heated assembly by men who ardently desire the legislation in their interest against men who ardently oppose it in their interest. The laws of the Islam are firmly based upon the *Shariah* and are, therefore, in the interest of the people as a whole. They are the work not of warring politicians, but of sober jurists.[1] Islamic law and *Shariah* was not revealed for limited application for a specific age. It suits every age and time. It will remain valid and shall continue to be, till the end of life on earth. Its injunctions were coined in such a manner that they are not affected by the lapse of time. They do not become obsolete, nor do their general principles and basic theories need to change or be revised. The generalized construction and elasticity of *Shariah* allows even for bringing under their jurisdiction, any unprecedented new case, even though it is not possible to expect its occurrence at the beginning of revelation.

Hence, the provisions of Islamic law and jurisprudence are not susceptible to change or substitution as are other laws and legislation. This is the "Divine beauty" and "Divine perfection" of Islamic law.[2] So, to the cynics who perceive Islamic law as hostile and barbaric, I challenge them to take the time to read and understand the spiritual, legal, political, social and economic vitality of Islamic law. In a world troubled by crisis after crisis, Islamic Law and Jurisprudence offers viable solutions and alternatives to the problems that mankind now encounters in the international political and economic arena. Islamic law is the most apposite tool to correct the injustices of our world. It must, however, be applied to suit current, conditions and complexities that exist in International Relations and Diplomacy.

2.2 The Madinah Chapter as a Model in International Relations

It is now a considered opinion among Islamic and non-Is-
lamic scholars that the Madinah Charter serves as both a relevant and inspirational guide in the field of global diplomatic
relations. As both a student and a practitioner of International
Law and Diplomacy, I am deeply moved and inspired by the
essence and practicability of the Madinah Charter. If the principles of this Charter were to be followed with the utmost sincerity by world leaders and international policy makers around
the globe, I can confidently say that human conflicts, whether
they be religious, political, economic, ethnic or social, would be
significantly reduced if not totally eliminated. Why would this
be so? The answer is quite simple. If "Divine Justice" was the
essence of man's relationship with his fellow men, this ideal
would subsequently transcend the realm of national and international affairs. But before I endeavor to go into the depth of the
Madinah Charter, I find it imperative once again to focus on the
person who initiated the Madinah Charter, that being the Holy
Prophet Muhammad (may peace be upon him). The Poet,
Lamartine, writes: "As regards all standards by which human
greatness may be measured, we may well ask: Is any man
greater than the Prophet Muhammad?"[3] Bernard Shaw once said
that, "If all the world was united under one leader, then
Muhammad would have been the best fitted man to lead the
peoples of various creeds, dogmas and ideas".[4] We may conclude by quoting Joseph Hell: "Muhammad is a great man without whom the world would have been incomplete. He initiated
and brought to fulfillment spiritual forces that would never have
come to birth without him. The extraordinary vitality of these
forces proves even today positively that the founder of Islam
belongs to the past and to the future, and to both so completely
that they cannot be distinguished from the present".[5]

Prophet Muhammad was an ideal leader of men. He was an
embodiment of all virtues; trustworthiness, sincerity, kindness,

14

affection, generosity and a great charm of mind and heart. Even his arch enemies recognized the noble qualities of his character and trusted him unhesitatingly. His affection for children, sympathy and kindness to the poor, the orphans and distressed knew no bounds. Magnanimity and forgiveness were the supreme qualities of his character. His forgiveness and generosity to the Jews is also unprecedented in history.

It is only when we know and understand the man Muhammad, that we can then appreciate the enduring model of the Madinah Charter in present day international relations and diplomacy. The essential principle of the Madinah Charter was that it sought to guarantee individual rights, irrespective of the religious beliefs of the communities, living in Madinah. In the building of the state, the Prophet introduced a political order based on the principle of equality for all. The prophet was a great democrat. The Commonwealth of Islam, he established at Madinah, was based on the democratic ideals of liberty, equality and fraternity. He gave absolute equality both to the Ansars and the Muhajjerins, though the latter represented the autocratic and ruling class of pre-Islamic Arabia. In the Commonwealth, the Prophet also granted the Jews and Christians full civic rights.

The Holy Prophet Muhammad (PBUH) initiated a policy of splendid religious tolerance to Jews and Christians. Their life and property were secured; their religion was not to be interfered with. Their prophets were to be respected. The charter that the Prophet gave to the Christians is a monument of fundamental citizens' rights and of enlightened toleration in an age of bitter religious discrimination and persecution. In this charter, the Prophet instructed his followers to help the Christians even in the repairs of their churches. Islam has ruled without coercion and propagated itself through gentleness, persuasion and conviction by argument alone.[6]

The foregoing political document which Muhammad documented fourteen centuries ago, establishes the freedom of faith and opinion, the inviolability of the city, human life and property and the forbiddance of crime. It certainly constitutes a breakthrough in the political and civil life of the world at that time. That age was one in which exploitation, tyranny and corruption were well established. Thus, Madinah and all the territories surrounding it became inviolate to their peoples who were now bound to rise to their defence and protection together. These people were now bound to guarantee one another in the implementation of the covenant, in the establishment of the rights arising therefrom, and in the provision of the freedom for which it had called.[7]

It is, with fervent hope, that I have articulated in form and substance, both the essence and practical objectives of the Madinah Charter. As a practising Muslim, I must confess that before I undertook the assignment of this research project I never fully appreciated the spiritual, political, social, moral and economic depth of the Madinah Charter. It is my humble opinion that this Chapter should be carefully studied by world leaders, foreign policy strategists, international law makers, politicians, statesmen and, last but not the least, by the Muslim Ummah. In this Charter, lies a model that could save all mankind from total annihilation. I confidently challenge the critics of Islam and Islamic law and jurisprudence who constantly strive to be the enemies of justice, fair play and equity in International Relations and global diplomacy by saying to them: "Go and study the Madinah Charter before passing reckless and irresponsible judgment." It is now a moral imperative that those at the helm of international organizations, such as the United Nations, should integrate the relevant areas of Madinah Charter into their own policy formulation and implementation. I now fully understand why President Bill Clinton of the United States, who came under severe pressure and criticism (nationally as well as internationally) because he invited Salman Rushdie, the author of the "Satanic Verses", to the White House in the name of free press said, "I have the greatest respect for the Islamic religion and the Islamic culture." Thus, no doubt, is a very wise, responsible and informed statement coming from the leader of the strongest nation in the world today.

Our planet earth is filled with trouble spots too numerous to mention. Many countries are plagued by the scourge of armed conflict, political and economic injustice. Mankind is consumed by a lust for enormous greed and power. We live in a world where people are no longer interested in the ideal of peaceful coexistence through mutual tolerance, but solely by material aspirations and the perpetual domination over their fellow human beings. Countries are primarily concerned with the political, economic, military, technological supremacy, and world diplomatic posture. Permanent interests remain the bedrock of their foreign policy formulation and implementation. However, this quest for selfish interests at both national and international levels have yielded results which have been no less than catastrophic. They have missed the essence of human existence on earth, which is the capacity for man to want for his brother what he wants for himself. Justice was not enacted to serve only the fortunate, but the less fortunate as well. The essence of the Madinah Charter was "enlightened tolerance". This pursuit of enlightened tolerance was initiated by Prophet Muhammad (PBUH), fourteen hundred years ago, in a time of great human turmoil. It serves as a model not only in the field of international relations and diplomacy, but also in the sphere of all human interaction.

"Until the day when there is no more first class and second class citizens, and equal rights and guaranteed for all, there will be war, nothing but war!"

These words were taken from a famous speech by Emperor Haile Selassie of Ethiopia. This profound message was eloquently delivered by the great Reggae superstar, the late Honourable Robert Nesta Marley (Bob Marley), O.M., who was a renowned son of the Caribbean island of Jamaica.

One may wonder why some Muslim countries do not appear to observe this charter, not only in relation to non-Muslim countries, but even between Muslim countries inter se, as may be illustrated by prosecution of the Iran-Iraq War (1979-1987) and the Persian Gulf War (1990-1991). It should, however, be appreciated that there is no perfection in human institutions or human relations. Nonetheless, it is to be hoped that with greater efforts, endurance and understanding, the Madinah Charter has a lasting message of peace and justice universally – to both Muslim and non-Muslim countries.

Chapter Three

The Future Impact of Islamic Law and Jurisprudence

3.1 The Future Impact of Islamic law and jurisprudence in Global Diplomatic Relations

Islamic law and jurisprudence has the potential of becoming a potent force in global diplomatic relations if a conductive atmosphere is given to it. To demonstrate a conducive atmosphere, let us use Nigeria for an example. The majority of the population in Nigeria are Muslims and their culture is guided by Islamic law. Nevertheless, Islamic law has no positive role within the socio-economic, legal and political environment. Take for instance, the legal system before colonialism in Northern Nigeria; Islamic law was the complete legal system, but the changes that the colonial masters introduced changed the then existing system. What remains now of the pre-colonial Islamic law is the matters of personal affairs, example, marriage, divorce, distribution of estate and some minor matters. The issue of contracts and agency has been taken away by common law. Before any meaningful and positive role can take place in the international legal system, there will be a definite need for trained and qualified legal practitioners in international law who are specialists in Islamic law and jurisprudence and who are also members of international bodies, such as the World Court and the United Nations. The question, therefore, is, will qualified international lawyers who specialize in Islamic law and jurisprudence, be allowed to represent Islamic interests in international relations and diplomacy? At the present time, there is no such trust. The issue, therefore, is a power tussle between the Western world and the Islamic world. Both the Western bloc and the Eastern bloc are all enemies of Islam. I would add that they are enemies because of ignorance and their constant quest to dominate and suppress the less fortunate occupants of planet earth. They are purely motivated by political, economic, military and techno-logical supremacy not by the noble ideals of equal rights, liberty, divine justice and morality. This is why our planet earth today is not a level playing field for all and sundry in interna-tional relations and diplomacy but, rather, a playing field for armed conflict, brute force and might over right.

I pose the following question: Will Islamic law and jurispru-dence emerge as a potent force in international affairs and global diplomacy given the new quest for human justice for all and sundry by such superpowers like the United States of America? If the United States of America is sincere to this claim, Islamic law will not only emerge as a potent force in international rela-tions and diplomacy, but it will guide and facilitate the achieve-ment of "human justice" for all and sundry. If this goal is realized, the future impact of Islamic law and jurisprudence in global diplomatic relations will play a positive role towards the future security and total well being of all mankind. I would like to add that justice in Islamic law is not human but "divine". See *Qur'an* 4:135 which states "Human life is made sacrosanct in Islam. Its inviolability has been affirmed in many verses of the *Qur'an* among which are the following: *"And kill not the soul which Allah has made sacrosanct, save for just cause".*[8]

Qur'an 5:8 also declares:
"O Ye who believe: Stand out firmly for justice as witnesses, for God, even as against yourselves, or your parents, or your kin, and whether it be (against) rich or poor, for God can best protect both. Follow not the lusts (of your hearts) lest ye swerve, and if you distort (justice) or decline to do justice, verily Allah is well acquainted with all that you do."[9]

20

I positively believe that both of these profound declarations from the Muslim Holy Book, the *Holy Qur'an*, form the basis for the improvement of future global diplomatic relations.

3.2 Can and will the Muslim Ummah effect meaningful change in Global Foreign Policy Formulation?

The answer to this question is, "Will they?"

Unfortunately, many Muslims in positions of political, social and economic influence, Islamic scholars and leaders of thought are tied to the legal, moral, political and economic status quo of their Western masters. Their selfish interests supersede their love for Almighty Allah's cause or this earth and in the hereafter. They operate on the notion of "permanent interests" not "permanent justice" for all and sundry. They have, whether they know it or not, become the worst enemies of their own religion.

However, the meaningful change in global policy formation will come from the "sincere" masses of the Muslim Ummah. They, with the help of Almighty Allah, are impacting positively in how foreign policy is formulated and implemented. Allah is giving them victory over their enemies. The growing Islamic culture and Islamic consciousness is brought about by the fervent desire of the sincere masses of the Muslim Ummah who seek a fairer and more just world. They are not tied to any Western master of Western status quo. They are motivated by the *Holy Qur'an* and the *Sunnah* of the Holy Prophet Muhammad (Peace be upon him). It is they who are now challenging injustices around the globe. They can and will effect meaningful change in foreign global policy formulation, because they are the ones who Almighty Allah has chosen to deliver mankind from the wrath of injustice, immorality, tyranny, oppression and ultimate destruction.

There are, however, some practical disabilities that confront the Muslim Ummah who advocate meaningful economic and social change in global foreign policy formulation. Technological and economic limitations are definite setbacks in this quest for equality, justice freedom and liberty for all mankind. Technological expertise and technological advancement are essential factors in foreign policy formulation. Only Islamic countries such as Pakistan, Egypt and Turkey have acquired the technological know-how that put them in a position of parity in global foreign policy formulation and implementation. So there needs to be a new thrust aimed at developing the technology of the Islamic world. There must be a thrust to ensure economic parity in the international economic environment. If this is attained whether in the short term or long term, the Muslim Ummah will no doubt lead to a dynamic and positive change in world affairs. It will further lead to a more active participation by Muslims in international political, economic and diplomatic decisions. Sincerity of purpose by Muslim and non-Muslim leaders around the globe, however, is the main ingredient for any effective and meaningful change in global foreign policy formulation and implementation. This sincerity of purpose must be translated into meaningful deeds, not mere empty promises and deceptive rhetorical utterances.

Chapter Four

Improving and Enhancing Global Communication and International Trade

4.1 The Improvement and Enhancement of Global Communication and International Trade via an understanding of a growing Islamic Culture.

A lack of understanding and familiarity with the business practices, social customs and etiquette of a country can weaken a country or a company's position in the international market place, prevent it from accomplishing its objectives and ultimately lead to failure. As business has become increasingly internationalized and global communications technology continues to develop, the need for clearly understood communications between members of different cultures is even more crucial.

Growing competition for international markets is another reason that companies must consider cultural distinctions. Business executives who are not alert to cultural differences simply cannot function in the international business arena. They may not even understand something as basic as what signifies closing a deal in a particular country – a handshake, a written contract or memorandum of understanding. Taking the time to learn the culture of the country, before doing business there, is a show of respect and is usually deeply appreciated, not to mention rewarding for the company. Countries and companies who understand different cultural differences are more likely to develop successful long-term relationships in international trade, international relations, international political and economic co-operation. I have vowed to give a thorough understanding in the area of international trade and global communication for the purpose of educating those in the corridors of political, economic or corporate power regarding the relevance and the importance of culture in international trade, international politics and global decision making. Now I will proceed to expand on the specific area of this which is the improvement and enhancement of global unification in international trade from an Islamic perspective. With a growing Islamic culture universally, it has now become imperative for the Western world not only to understand and appreciate Islamic culture, but also to respect it. Why is this? It is so because the Islamic world today has enormous economic strength and economic potential. Many Islamic countries and their citizens, for example, have huge investments in the United States of America and Europe. These huge investments have made them powerful brokers in international business decisions.

Unfortunately, however, many of these power brokers who are Muslims, have conveniently decided not to promote the growing Islamic culture, but, rather, they have decided to join forces with the Western status quo. This is just the stark reality. What is culture? Culture is a complex phenomenon. It is subject to several definitions and capable of being viewed from many angles.[10] But, simply stated, it can be defined as the sum total of a peoples' way of life. Culture consists of values, beliefs and perceptions of the world that underlie a people's behaviour and which are shared by members of a particular society. It is that aspect of our existence that makes us similar to some people yet different from other peoples of the world. The distinction between "us" and "them" is largely a matter of culture. Culture is acquired. It is learned through the medium of language over a period of time. It is not inherited nor is it acquired by instinct. The fact that culture has to be learnt or acquired is important in understanding why people behave and react to events the way they do. After the process of learning, culture becomes an integral part of the daily lives of individuals. It is in the process of learning that people inculcate the complex whole that culture is. Culture is not static; it is, rather, very dynamic. It is a phenomenon that responds to changes arising from developments within particular societies.[11]

Now that we have defined what culture is, we now are in a better position to comprehend the subject matter of this specific area of interest. It is in light of this, that we propose, that if international trade and global communication is to be truly dynamic and mutually beneficial to all of its players, there needs to be more respect and tolerance in respect of a growing Islamic culture. One cannot ignore the numerical strength of 1.3 billion Muslims around the globe. Their numerical, spiritual, economic and political strength will not suddenly vanish from our planet Earth. Many nations have found it necessary for their own political, economic and technological survival to understand American diplomacy. But before one understands American diplomacy, one has to understand the American culture. Similarly, before one can understand Islamic diplomacy, one has to make a fervent attempt at understanding the Islamic religion and its tenets.

Incidentally, the Islamic religion and Islamic culture do not operate in isolation from each other, rather, they operate in total harmony and unison. As the world community has now moved into the 21st century, and as planet Earth becomes a global village of mutual interdependence, mutual co-operation and mutual respect, the understanding of growing Islamic culture is a necessity for improved and enhanced global communication. Similarly, as the world becomes a global market place, and expanded international trade is the engine of growth for economies around the world, whether they may be developed or developing, more attention and tolerance must be given to the growing Islamic culture. Economic considerations remain the number one priority of nations and corporations around the globe. It is in their "Permanent Interest". They should, therefore, ardently strive for a better understanding of the growing

Islamic culture. This will not only improve and enhance global communication and international trade, but it also makes good business sense.

4.2   THE DYNAMIC RELATIONSHIP BETWEEN TRADE AND THE RELIGION OF ISLAM

I find it most appropriate to quote one of the most profound statements of the Holy Prophet Muhammad (may peace be upon him), which says:

"Work in pursuit of your worldly life as if you are living forever, and work in pursuit of the life in the hereafter as if you are dying tomorrow."

This articulate message exemplifies the balance and moderation in the Islamic religion in respect of trade and commerce. Islam, as some misguided people are led to believe, is not anti-trade or anti-business; it is, rather, pro-trade and probusiness. Recently, I had the opportunity to visit Kano State in Nigeria and held meaningful and productive discussions with some Islamic scholars and Islamic traditional rulers. They made me understand that Islam came to the Northern Region of Nigeria through trade. It did not come offering a hopeful pie in the sky when you die. It came in the form of trade and commerce. This discovery was very enlightening for me as it broadened my horizon about Islam. The early traders in Northern Nigeria used trade to propagate Islam. This seemed very interesting but, more so, very practical indeed. A wise man once said: "Before you talk to a hungry man about God and religion, feed him first". Islam does not operate independently from man's socio-economic and biological needs. The messenger of Allah, Prophet Muhammad (PBUH), engaged in trade on behalf of Lady Khadijah, his first wife, and encouraged business through his own practice. He once said: "A trustworthy and an honest and truthful business-man will rise up with the martyrs on the day of Resurrection".[12] In yet another Hadith, he has said: "A truthful and trustworthy trader will rise up with the Prophets, the righteous and the martyrs."[13]

So it is time to dispel the notion that trade and commerce is contrary to the Islamic religion. It certainly is not. The relationship is one of vitality and dynamism. Again, all that Islam requires in the areas of trade, commerce and business dealings is what it requires in all of the other facets of the religion is that of honesty, straight-forward dealing, justice, equity and mutual respect. Trade in all forms must be clean and honest. If one carries it out according to the guidance of the *Qur'an* and the *Sunnah*, he or she will see Allah's blessings even though fabulous wealth may not be amassed.

After all, as the Holy Prophet has said, nine parts out of ten of one's recommended livelihood lies in trade and commerce. As long as there is no tyranny, deceit, hoarding, cut-throat competition, transaction involving usury, every Muslim is encouraged to do trade and business. The only trade that is declared unlawful *HARAM* is that of dealing in wine and other intoxicants, pigs and things made out *of* it, idols and images. Abubakar, Umar and other companions of the Prophet were engaged in lawful trade at one time or the other in their lives. All that is required *of* the trader or businessman in Islam is that one's livelihood be earned in a lawful manner. It does not stipulate that one must not earn a profit. Rather, Islam encourages lawful profit. Islam is not a critic of "honest capitalism". It only asks that the capitalist be just and have a conscience in matters of trade, commerce, property and contractual dealings. Unfortunately, however, many Muslims and non-Muslims alike succumb to the lusts and greed of their hearts, thus distorting the real spiritual and moral essence of Allah's intention for all humanity. Islamic economic philosophy emphasizes the importance of "trade", not "aid". This dynamic relationship between trade and commerce and the religion of Islam is one of "Divine Perfection". This relationship is a positive model that could no doubt bring about lasting and viable solutions in the complex area of international trade and world economic development.

27

Chapter Five

The Potential Impact of Islamic Law and Jurisprudence

5.1 The Potential impact of Islamic Law and Jurisprudence in the New World Political and Economic Order

In the New World, Political and Economic Order, Islamic law and jurisprudence can have impact if the leaders of thought can give room to accommodate Islamic ideas. The Islamic Political and Economic Order is accommodating to other political and economic views. There is no imposition or oppression. In economic affairs, the world could emulate the Islamic market economy system with all the restrictions placed upon means of creating artificial inflation and corruption. The Islamic market economy operates on the basis of economic justice.

The influence of leaders of thought will vary from country to country. These leaders of thought can influence and in some instances manipulate the political directorate in the making of public policy in the political, social and economic arena. Islamic ideas could definitely enhance the policy making process in both economic and political affairs. The goal of Islamic law is to have a social, economic and political order based on the principle of "Human Justice" for all mankind.

In the area of world trade, for example, Islamic law and jurisprudence encourages mutual cooperation and mutual interest. On that basis if one is contributing ten percent, will the profit be ten percent? The capitalist is not allowed to dictate his or her terms to the labourer. The issue we must decide on is how much is being contributed and how much is being gained. One of the primary objectives of the Islamic Economic Order is that there is no relationship of master-servant, but partner versus partner. Beyond that, Islam gives more recognition of labour than to capital. So any capital that could not participate in labour or in risk is not entitled to get any share of the profit. That is why the doctrine of Usury (RIBA) is conceived as unlawful *(Haram)* under Islamic law. Another means of discouraging saving of the capital is matter of charity *(Zakat)*; if you refuse to invest your capital, *Zakat* may usurp it.

A proper understanding of the economic system in Islam, will offer a better perspective, or the potential impact and possible role Islamic law and jurisprudence will play in the New World Political and Economic Order. The goals and values of an Islamic economic system are:-

a) Economic well-being within the framework of moral norms of Islam;

b) Universal brotherhood and justice;

c) Equitable distribution of income and wealth; and

d) Freedom of the individual within the context of social welfare.

This list of goals is by no means complete, but should provide a sufficient framework for discussing and elaborating the Islamic economic and political views within the context of any meaningful New World Political Economic Order.[14] The concept of brotherhood and equal treatment of all individuals in society and the law is not meaningful, unless accompanied by economic justice so that everyone will get his due contribution to the social product and that there is no exploitation of individual by another. The Prophet aptly warned: "Beware of injustice for injustice will be equivalent to darkness on the day judgment". This warning against injustice and exploitation is designed to protect the rights of all individuals in society (whether consumers or producers and distributors, and whether employers or employees) and to promote general welfare. For any new world political and economic order to be meaningful, the incorporation of Islamic ideas is a moral, social, and economic imperative. This then is the ultimate goal.

Islamic law and jurisprudence has the potential to play a dynamic and meaningful role in the New World Political and Economic order if leaders of thought become sensitized by the Islamic principles of justice, equality, mutual tolerance, mutual co-operation and mutual respect. If leaders of thought are inspired by these principles, we will, without a doubt have a "safer" and "secure" world. If however, they continue to be guided by permanent interests, supremacy and domination over fellow human beings or nations, Islamic law will face a very difficult and formidable challenge.

There are, however, other critical factors that will definitely impede the potential impact of Islamic law and jurisprudence, in the New World Political and Economic Order.[15] Most Muslim countries have been unable to internalize the engine of growth. Their economies are dependent on the western capitalist countries in a number of ways – for the import of foodstuffs, manufactured goods, technology, etc., on the one hand, and for export of their primary products on the other. Some of them are suffering from the effect of lingering legacies of colonial economic relationships and appear as perfect examples of a "centre periphery" relationship. The paradox of the Muslim world is that it is resource-rich, but economically poor and weak. Development planning has been introduced in a number of Muslim countries. In some, the art is now at a fairly advanced level. Nigeria, Egypt, Syria, Algeria, Iran, Pakistan, Malaysia, Indonesia are some of the instances. But in almost all these countries, developmental effort is modeled after the prototypes of growth developed by the western theorists and practitioners of planning and "sold" to the planners in the Muslim countries via international diplomacy, economic pressurization, intellectual infiltration and a number of other overt and covert means.[16]

The Islamic concept of human and world development has a comprehensive character and includes moral, spiritual and ma-

30

terial aspects. Development becomes a goal-and-value-oriented activity devoted to the optimization of human well-being in all these dimensions. The moral and material, the economic, political and the social, the spiritual and the physical are inseparable. It is not merely welfare in this world that is the objective. The welfare and Islam seeks to extend to the life hereafter and there is no conflict between the two. This dimension is at present missing in the contemporary concept of human and world development. This dimension is also missing in the much talked about "New World Economic Order."[17]

Many western scholars have sought to misrepresent and misinterpret Islamic law and jurisprudence. They have manipulated world political and economic opinion by portraying Islamic law and jurisprudence as some ancient, barbaric, uncivilized and backward philosophical ideal that will turn the clock back for human progress. But little do they know that they are responsible for the present state of confusion in our world today. Little do they know they are the uncivilized oppressors of "suffering humanity". Islamic law and jurisprudence despite unfavourable world opinion and conditions will definitely have not only a potential impact on the New World Political and Economic Order, but will ultimately take centre stage as suffering humanity cries out desperately for their salvation from the injustices perpetuated by unkind and unjust oppressors.

I fervently pray for a world guided by the Islamic philosophy and principle of mutual cooperation, not useless confrontation. With mutual cooperation, a new partnership will definitely emerge amongst nation states, whether they may be big or small, rich or poor, developed or developing. A new attitude of mutual trust and a sense of belonging to one earth will also be achieved. Let us try and understand that mankind has a common destiny aimed at the attainment of the noble ideals of justice, peace, unity, equity, brotherhood and international love. If the proposed new world order is to have any meaningful impact for mankind's future humanity, it must be guided by these tenets.

Chapter Six

Can Human Justice Become A Reality?

6.1   Can Human Justice become a reality in present day International Affairs?

It is possible for human justice to prevail and even become more of a reality if these pre-conditions are created:-

i.   Justice that goes beyond more technicalities and procedures;

ii. Justice that is accessible to all the sundry without any financial hindrances or modalities;

iii. Impartial judges to be placed in appropriate places in the international legal system and in international organizations.

However, the realization of these goals will not be an easy task. Why? Because those persons in the corridors of political, economic and military power are not just going to wake up and have a sincere change of heart for the less fortunate of this world. This is the exact reason why revolutions are born, not because the masses are evil, but because they see revolution as the only way for them to escape the wrath of tyranny, injustice and oppression.

Present day international affairs are motivated not by "human justice" but rather by "permanent interests". Many nation-states today have made their national and international interests the end all and be all of their foreign policy objectives. That gives rise to the foreign policy philosophy "no permanent friends", no "permanent enemies," only "permanent interests". As a practicing Muslim actively engaged in international relations and diplomacy and foreign policy strategies, I am by no means proposing that nation states should disregard or relegate their national and international interests merely for the sake of utopian ideals. What I advocate, however, is that human welfare and survival on this earth should be seen as being paramount, above any permanent national or international interests. If our human survival and existence on earth becomes threatened, what then is the value of selfish permanent interests?

If there is no justice on this earth, there will never be any peace, and, if there is no peace, the national or international interest of nation-states will not serve any meaningful purpose for their own corporate existence. Unfortunately, many foreign policy experts remain blind to the most relevant aspect of human interaction, whether it may be on the national or international level, that being "human justice" for all and sundry. They would cynically respond that "human justice" is merely a story book fairy tale. The only time that they will respond favourably to the cause of human justice is when their own national and international political, economic and technological survival is at stake.

I cite, for example, the case of Bosnia. The super powers, such as the United States of America and Great Britain, are apparently insensitive to the atrocities arising out of ethnic rivalries in Bosnia. This atrocity against Bosnian Muslims does not inspire them to take resolute and forceful action whether it be economic or military. Why is this so? The answer is very simple. Bosnia is not a strategically and economically important country to them. It is not the life of young American military men and women. There is not oil interest at state as in the case of Kuwait. The much promoted "Operation Desert Storm" and "Liberation of Kuwait" was not about human justice or human sanctity, but rather about maintaining and preserving America's economic and political interests in the Persian Gulf region. If the presentation of the Muslims in Bosnia meant the continued economic and political supremacy of the United States of America and Great Britain, I can confidently say that more purposeful action would have been taken from the onset of this human tragedy.

It is in light of these developments that this book suggests that for human justice to become a reality in present day international affairs, a new version of "humanism" must become the priority of world leaders and leaders of thought universally. Former American President, Jimmy Carter, said: "The life of a black African is not seen as important as that of the life of a white European". This remark was in response to questions concerning the various trouble spots around the globe.

Both the United Nations and the International Court of Justice must now seriously re-examine their crucial role in international relations, international law and diplomatic intercourse. They must, as a matter of moral and human imperative, respond to the rapid changes in the international political and economic environment. They cannot afford to remain static in their policy making formulation. There is, at present, a new and vibrant thrust amongst the less fortunate citizens of the world, who are now fighting for "parity", not everlasting "charity".

Islam actively promotes the doctrine of "absolute justice" in all aspects of human endeavour. Besides, Islam teaches that God is the ultimate judge, that His scale is that of absolute justice, a scale which loses not an atom's weight of good works, or an atom's weight of evil works (Qur'an 99:7-8); a scale which admits of no intercession by any one, no favouritism to any one.[18]

As mankind enters the horizon of the twenty-first century, human justice will not only become a reality in international affairs, but it will also change the focus of foreign policy experts around the globe, not by choice, but more so by necessity. International relations and global diplomacy is now a dynamic process. The pendulum has swung. The rich nations can no longer totally dictate to the poor nations; territorial sovereignty is a right for all. Yes, material domination through economic and technological supremacy still actively exists. However, it is no longer seen as an exclusive birthright for the continued manipulation and exploitation of the poorer nations.

It is difficult for historians to recall a period when the world has experienced such rapid and cataclysmic changes as have occurred during the past five years. Which diplomat, economist, pundit, journalist or seer now boldly claims to have predicted the fall of the Berlin Wall, the disintegration of the Soviet Union, the collapse of the communist empire, the recent peace accord between Israel and the Palestine Liberation Organization (PLO), or the disappearance of the abhorrent system of racial injustice known to all as apartheid in South Africa?[19]

Asked what caused the fall of communism in Eastern Europe, President Lech Walesa is reported to have turned to a nearby television set and aptly stated: "It all came from here!" The words of Herodotus remain as true today as when first uttered in Greek over 2000 years ago: "Nothing endures, but change". These words of wisdom should become the guiding philosophy in international affairs.

President Nelson Mandela's rise to the helm of government in South Africa is a living testimony that the noble Islamic ideals of "human justice" and "absolute justice", whether it be in national or international affairs, is alive and well. It is not longer a myth. It never was.

It has been said that there can be no peace without justice. The welcome end of the "cold war" enables the global community to fulfill at last the dreams which have so long eluded us: a planet where hunger and famine no longer exist, where disease, ignorance and the scourge of poverty are removed. Only then will there be human justice on earth – only then can there be a lasting peace.[20]

It is with sincere hope that a brighter future will be realized for mankind to inhabit one world that is single and indivisible. This goal is attainable. Let us seize the opportunity – the time and the place is right here on earth.

Chapter Seven

Muhammad Ali

As I endeavour to conclude this section, I find it most appropriate to focus on the person from whom I have drawn both my spiritual and human inspiration and motivation, my personal mentor, friend and Muslim brother, the former three-time heavyweight world champion, the most recognized human being on the planet and most of all the most loved person in the world, that being no other person than Muhammad Ali. Muhammad Ali was the people's champion inside the ring and still remains the people's champion outside the ring. He is the perfect embodiment of the spirit of man.

Time and time, again Muhammad Ali has been an international goodwill Ambassador Extraordinary, always promoting the cause of peace and justice. Muhammad Ali once profoundly stated:

"War on nations change maps. War on poverty maps change."

One would never expect wisdom of this kind to come from a great fighter and athlete, rather it is expected to come from a prudent foreign policy expert. Most foreign policy experts, however, lack this kind of spiritual and human depth. That is exactly why the world is in the condition it is in today.

Muhammad Ali's life has now entered a new and exciting dimension outside the boxing ring. He humorously states:

"In the ring I floated like a butterfly, and I stung like a bee, then I made boxing history, but now I am fighting to save humanity."

As he declared to one of his many attentive audiences in the Sudan:

"My real career started after my retirement from the ring. Almighty God, Allah, by making me famous through boxing, has blessed me with the opportunity to face the even bigger challenges of poverty, hunger, discrimination, ignorance and other human miseries."

He is now fighting injustice, fighting racism, fighting crime, fighting illiteracy, fighting poverty, using the face that the world knows so well, to fight for truth and different causes around the globe. "The whole world is in trouble", says Ali.

"Crime is on the rise, the environment is deteriorating, you've got people fighting and the threat of nuclear war, no long-term friendships, corruption in government, evangelist preachers doing things they shouldn't do; no respect for elders; prejudice and injustice; people highjacking planes, Jews and Muslims in the Middle East and Protestants and Catholics in Northern Ireland fighting each other. What's the reason? What's the cause? There's peace and tranquility among the animals. There's peace and tranquility among the animals. Everything in nature is in perfect order except man. Man is suffering because he has adopted a way of life that is against nature and the laws of God." Ali further states:

"All this hating in the world is wrong. Forget about nations. Forget about colour. Forget about different religion. People are people; God created us all. The only thing that makes one man better than another is the goodness of his deeds in the eyes of God. And only God can judge deeds. It is not for another man to judge. Here in this great country America – we have been making progress on how people get along. But there is a lot of hatred, and hating someone because of his skin colour is wrong not only in Islam, but it is wrong, period. It is wrong both ways; it doesn't matter which colour does the hating. All people, all races, all colours, must work together for the total harmony of all mankind. We must fight hunger in the world, hunger isn't just being hungry. It means you feel sick. We must fight homelessness. People shouldn't sleep on the streets. It is wrong. I would go to some place like the Sudan, and when I get back to America I would be asked questions about what I experienced, or what I saw. I would say I saw children starving to death. That is what I saw. Yes. Young innocent babies starving to death."[21]

Ali's support for many causes to help the less fortunate is not only verbal and financial, but also the sacrifice of his time for direct work and involvement is clear proof of the seriousness and sincerity of his words. Ali's deeds are nothing less than exemplary. Countless honours have been stowed upon him worldwide – by millions of people around the globe who fondly call him "World Hero".

One may ask: What is the relevance of Muhammad Ali to this thesis? I say it is perfectly relevant. Most of the problems that plague mankind today are articulately expressed by him. He has traveled and met with more world leaders, Presidents, Heads of States and Prime Ministers, than any other person on earth. He discusses international affairs and world events not merely from a superficial perspective, but rather from a spiritual, moral, intellectual and human perspective. I thank God for giving me the privilege to have encountered such a special human being. It is a life long experience of positive spiritual and moral inspiration. If one understands the in-depth thoughts of this great man, it would immediately dispel all the ridiculous and biased notions of the Islamic religion and by extension Islamic law and jurisprudence.

It would be most apposite to describe Muhammad Ali, one of the most popular Muslims in the world, as a fanatic for "love", "peace" and "justice". Ali's life is an example of "human justice" for all and sundry. He has lived that creed. I sincerely believe that as the world sees a "new generation" of leaders who have an enlightened vision in their world views, Islamic law and jurisprudence will become more relevant in present day national relations and diplomacy.

The United States of America, for example, has had the good fortune to experience a President and a Vice President from a more enlightened generation. This, of course, does not mean that American foreign policy is going to make a sudden change towards human justice and parity in world affairs. It will not. What it means, however, if only at the present time merely a symbolic gesture, is that new leaders who are from a younger and more enlightened generation (in terms of their world view) will inspire a new thinking for other world leaders and leaders of thought in national relations and diplomacy to emulate.

International political and economic relations is at the present time at a crossroad between a lasting peace or perpetual misery for the occupants of our planet Earth. Once again, technological advancement, by itself, cannot and will not save our world. Material prosperity for a privileged few, cannot and will not save a corrupt and inhuman free market economy; and will not save our world from economic misery. Only a "new vision" will inspire the ideals of peace, justice, equal rights, economic parity, mutual co-operation, mutual respect and mutual tolerance for all our fellowmen will be the salvation for mankind, regardless of race, creed, colour, ethnicity or status in life.

The future emergence of Islamic law and jurisprudence in International Relations and Diplomacy will inspire this "new vision". As mankind has entered the threshold of the twenty-first century, it is with sincere hope that the goal of a lasting peace, human justice and world harmony will be the criteria for any New world Political and Economic Order. The time has now come for a serious reflection as we prepare to meet the difficult tasks ahead. At the present time, what we have in international affairs is a "New World Disorder". Fancy rhetorical discourse cannot change the fate of man. Sincerity of purpose will!

The Muslim Ummah must be prepared to face the difficult challenges that lie ahead and must be resolutely determined to put into action positive Islamic ideals. Muslims must strive to make themselves the envy of the world, practicing with sincerity what the *Holy Qur'an* prescribes and the practice of the *Sunnah* of the Holy Prophet Muhammad (may peace be upon him). If they successfully meet these challenges, Islamic law and jurisprudence will subsequently not only be relevant in present day

International Relations and Diplomacy but will eventually play a more decisive role in world affairs.

I close this discussion with the saying of a very wise man who once said: "Man can only advance to perfection, he can never attain it." The true and sincere practice of Islamic law and jurisprudence can indeed bring about perfection on this earth. It will at least offer moral, pragmatic and viable solutions to human, national and international conflicts. It will also bring about a more harmonious world which is essential to human well-being and human progress. Fervent attempts should, therefore, be made to advance to the attainment of "Islamic ideals". Once again, Muslims all over the universe must be prepared to face the challenges of the future, by advancing to perfection. The attainment of these Islamic ideals, by Muslims and non-Muslims alike, in international affairs and global policy making, will assist in correcting the present injustices in the international political and economic system and preserve human life on our plant Earth. It is within our grasp. Yes! A world motivated by the human ideal of "ONE LOVE, ONE HEART" (a la Bob Marley), is definitely within our grasp. The key to human salvation on earth is in the palms of our hands. We should all faithfully grasp it – GIVE PEACE AND JUSTICE A CHANCE NOW!

Chapter 8

The Message and the Solution is Divine Justice

As-Salaamu-Alaikum (Peace Be Unto You)

Contrary to world misconception and distortion, Islam is not based on nationalism, tribal glory, insane fanaticism, intolerance or racial superiority. The fundamental principles of Islam are about peace and compassion for all and enlightened tolerance. These noble ideals were taught and practised by our beloved Holy Prophet Muhammad (May Peace Be Upon Him). Human kindness, generosity and universal love and brotherhood are the fundamental tenets of both Islam and Christianity.

Islam is not to be perceived as, an Arab 'thing', an Indian 'thing', a Black 'thing', an African 'thing', or a White 'thing', or some dogmatic culture. The essence and purity of Islam is about spiritual, moral, and economic upliftment and salvation of greater humanity through the sacred principle of Divine Justice for the entire human family.

Divine Justice is not subject to the whims and fancies and the human imperfections of mankind. Divine Justice, therefore, is superior to human justice as it comes from our Creator (Allah) and was revealed to the Holy Prophet Muhammad (May Peace Be Upon Him) during his time of Prophethood. Our beloved Holy Prophet (ISA) Jesus Christ (May Peace Be Upon Him) also fervently taught and practised the righteousness of Divine Justice.

If our world were governed by the sacred principles of Divine Justice the scourge of poverty, racism, human misery, hopelessness, homelessness, social and economic injustice, ignorance, greed intolerance, wars, and material indecency would no longer be a plague for the survival of suffering humanity.

Divine Justice, therefore, is now the only cure for a humanity that has lost its soul. Man's inhumanity to man has created the intolerable disease of **"World Injustice"**. Divine Justice is not merely an ideal for Muslims, or Christians, or Jews, or for the people of any particular religious faith. It is an ideal that must be enshrined in the bosom of the entire human race.

Divine Justice, my beloved brothers and sisters, is the only righteous and practical vision that can, and will inspire the noble ideals of Universal Love, a renewed hope and a lasting world peace for all the occupants of our planet Earth. We all are one. Let us now strive to make this dream of universal oneness an attainable reality for achieving the goal of a common humanity. With a common humanity, my beloved brothers and sisters, the Word is Love.

As-Salaamu-Alaikum (Peace Be Unto You)

"'All Praise is due to Allah', I bear witness that there is no God but Allah, the One, having no partner with Him. He fulfilled His promise and granted victory to His bondsman, and He alone routed the confederates (of the enemies of Islam)."

"O People listen to my words, for I do not know whether we shall ever meet again and perform Hajj after this year. O ye people, Allah says: O people we created you from one male and one female and made you into tribes and nations, so as to be known to one another. Verily in the sight of Allah, the most honoured amongst you is the one who is most God-fearing. There is no superiority for an Arab over a non-Arab and for a non-Arab over an Arab, nor for the white over the black nor the black over the white except by piety and good action."

As the world staggers into the 21st century, the spirit and principles of the Madinah Charter have enduring relevance to-day as a blue-print for world peace and global oneness. The noble ideals of peace, justice, equity and fair play, are attainable through an understanding and application of Islamic law and jurisprudence. As the esteemed author, Bernard Shaw, once said: "The wonderful vitality of Islam makes it supreme in all aspects of human interaction and endeavaour."

We presently live in a demented world motivated by the futility of domination and the arrogance of power, rather than the humanity of love. We live in a world not guided by the noble tenets and ideals of divine justice, equality, truth, morality, integrity and fair play, but rather in a world misguided by the philosophy and practice of permanent, self and myopic economic and political interests. Our Holy Prophet Muhammad (May Peace Be Upon Him), left an indelible legacy of human decency for mankind and it is now the challenge and the duty of the sincere Muslim Ummah to restore this great legacy. The time has come for us to dispel the notion that Islam is a religion of fanatics and goat herders. The time has come for us *to* show the world that Islam more than any other religion has the potential to prepare the world for sustainable peaceful economic and political growth in the 21st century and beyond. The time has come to carry forth the banner of Islam for universal peace and global oneness.

Dreamers dream, but when you fulfill your dream you become a missionary. Let us all keep the message of our Holy Prophet Muhammad (May Peace Be Upon Him) alive, a philosophy of universal love, divine justice, universal brotherhood, mutual tolerance, world peace, enlightened diplomacy and global oneness. As world citizens, we have both a challenge and a duty to restore sanity to a world that is indeed gone mad. A world that is gone mad with material indecency, greed and lust for spiritual, economic and political power.

There is great triumph and boasting of technological supremacy, and military power. However, there is not enough sincerity of purpose towards the acquisition of the "Power of Love." The greatest universal campaign that should be enacted with immediate effect is "Operation Love."

I suggest that International relations and diplomacy is not some mystique practice endowed upon some privileged class of persons. Diplomatic relations begins at the inter-personal level, even before it gets to the national and international level.

Going back home to "Mother Africa" is a life experience that I will always cherish, as this profound experience rekindled in me the common bonds of universal brotherhood and indeed strengthened my rich African ancestral desire. My many positive experiences in Nigeria is the culmination of a life long dream. My sojourn in Nigeria is the first step in what I hope will become a global mission of reconciliation and reconstruction through Islam. I did not acquire the difficult skills of diplomatic practice by merely being a Post Graduate student of International Law and Diplomacy at the University of Lagos; my greatest teachers of practical diplomacy were my brothers and sisters in Nigeria. Why is this so? This is so because, although I am of African descent, I had to adjust to a totally different culture. I had to adjust to several changes in cultural practices, different values and traditions and to different languages. I may humorously add, I even had to adjust to being stricken many times by malaria. Some of my best friends that I have made for life were found in Nigeria. I felt more at home there than any place that I have even lived or visited. In reflection, however, I became an integral part of the Nigerian family because I went there with an open mind and pure heart. This attitude enhanced my patience and tolerance and subsequently, prepared me for a very rich experience not only at the university or in the mosque, but more so, with many Nigerians from all walks of life. I may also add, that the essence and foundation for good diplomatic relations, is mutual tolerance and patience. Large and small countries alike must now subscribe to these simple but yet, profound principles. The disease of intolerance should become the greatest enemy of mankind. I will now endeavor to focus briefly on Nigeria-Jamaica Relations.

Jamaica and Nigeria have both enjoyed cordial and positive diplomatic relations for over twenty years.

During this period, both these countries have extended the hand of brotherhood and mutual friendship by offering moral and material support. Jamaica, in particular, has been the recipient of Nigeria's kind generosity and goodwill in specific areas, such as, oil agreements and technical aid programs. Incidentally, when the island of Jamaica was ravaged by Hurricane Gilbert in 1988, the Government of Nigeria was the largest single cash contributor to hurricane relief efforts. They were also many Nigerian doctors, nurses and teachers contributing positively to the welfare of many deprived Jamaicans through the Technical Aid Core programme.

However, in early 1996, diplomatic relations between Jamaica and Nigeria fell to an all time low following the execution of Ken Saro Wiwa and eight others convicted of murder charges. The Jamaican Government joined the Commonwealth of Nations and imposed sanctions against Nigeria. Jamaica's action against Nigeria were, by and large, a symbolic gesture, as it did not have any meaningful effect on Nigeria's economic or political programme.

Subsequently, Nigeria withdrew its technological and economic aid program and volunteers from Jamaica. Many innocent Jamaicans were severely hurt by this great loss, especially the departure of the caring nurses who integrated themselves into the Jamaican community. However, there has been a new thrust to try and heal some of the wounds between both countries. A high level delegation from Jamaica went to Nigeria and held what I think were useful and positive discussions with a view of normalizing diplomatic relations in the near future. I was personally told by a high level Jamaican government official, that the talks generated a new spirit of mutual respect between Jamaica and Nigeria. Let us all hope that this new spirit of mutual respect will translate into a new beginning between both countries. When countries mismanage their international affairs with other countries, it is the innocent people who suffer the results of that mismanagement. Nigeria, despite its shortcomings, is still the undisputed "Giant of Africa" and should be accorded this deserved respect by its allies, as well as, its adversaries. Jamaica too, is also the "Giant of the Caribbean" region in terms of its posture and its notable contributions to economic, political, social and cultural developments. We, therefore, should unite with one common bond and vision. The vision of course, should be international liberation. Before I move to the next discussion, I would like to note, for the purpose of giving vivid examples, the practice of diplomacy. In 1996, I hosted the Saudi Arabian Olympic National Athletic Track team, who visited Jamaica as part of an international delegation for the annual event of the Mutual Games. I also hosted a dinner reception for the Nigerian Ambassador to Cuba and Mexico, His Excellency Ambassador Yahaya Alhassan. On both occasions, our people interacted very positively, Muslims and non-Muslims alike. This was my own attempt in bringing Jamaica closer together once again with Nigeria and, in the case of Saudi Arabia, it was to develop a new and lasting friendship with another member of the Global Village. This is where practical diplomacy begins. It begins and ultimately ends at the personal level. When governments are at loggerheads with each other, their people must still peacefully coexist as members of the human family. This is all a part of the global mission of building bridges of understanding, humanity and hope.

I will now discuss Nigeria's role in African affairs. In 1975, Nigeria took a lead in establishing the Economic Community of West African States, ECOWAS. The organization's sixteen members range from Mauritania in the West to Nigeria herself and it includes countries once colonies of Britain, France and Portugal, as well as Liberia. ECOWAS' objective is the creation of a great area of free trade and movement in the West African area, to achieve which member states are prepared to concede the same degree of sovereignty as are the members of the EEC. Nigeria sees ECOWAS as essential, if West Africa as a whole is to become "self reliant" and the weaker states are to be free from external pressure and domination control. Here are some truths. It was Nigeria's leadership that made the difference in Liberia. It was

Nigeria which sent about 12,000 soldiers, shouldering the huge peacekeeping bill of close to $4 billion. Until today, close to 90% of peace keepers in Liberia are Nigerians. Nigeria played a very positive and pivotal role in terms of both moral and material support in bringing the Apartheid regime to its knees and ultimately its senses what little they had left. How then can Nigeria's contributions be ignored in respect of its own dynamic role in the stabilization of the African continent? Admittedly, Nigeria has made mistakes and squandered opportunities, but this in no way diminishes their contributions not only to the African continent, but to world affairs. Unless the United States of America gives due recognition to the largest black nation on earth, how can any meaningful Africa policy succeed? If President Bill Clinton wants to know why a good idea, such as the United States African Crisis Response Force faltered, he would find it in America's arrogance with respect to Nigeria.

Let me now turn to Nigeria and the international community. Before I do this, however, I would like to reiterate Nigeria's many contributions in the sphere of not only African Affairs, but also its dynamic participation in international relations. I have been fortunate and indeed blessed to have had the opportunity to be exposed to some of the best intellectual minds on the continent of Africa while living in Nigeria. It is this exposure that enhanced my own intellectual facility and improved my grasp of political, economic and social complexities entirely of not only Nigeria, but other African countries, primarily in the Sub-Sahara region. Once again, this served as enlightenment with respect to Nigeria and its posture in world politics.

Chapter 9

The Role of the United Nations in the pursuit of Global Justice

Let me now turn to the role and the responsibility of the United Nations Organization in the campaign for the achievement of Universal Divine Justice.

Article 1

"The purposes of the United Nations are:

1. To maintain international peace and security, and to that end: to take effective collective measures for the prevention and removal of threats to the peace, and for the suppression of acts of aggression or other breaches of the peace, and to bring about by peaceful means, and in conformity with the principles of justice and international law, adjustment or settlement of international disputes or situations which might lead to a breach of the peace;

2. To develop friendly relations among nations based on respect for the principle of equal rights and self-determination of peoples, and to take other appropriate measures to strengthen universal peace;

3. To achieve international co-operation in solving international problems of an economic, social, cultural or humanitarian character, and in promoting and encouraging respect for human rights and for fundamental freedoms for all without distinction as to race, sex, language or religion; and

4. To be a centre for harmonizing the actions of nations in the attainment of these common ends."

I close this segment with a focus on human rights and extreme poverty adopted in the United Nations General Assembly on December 23, 1994. [Meeting 1994] "Recognizing that the existence of widespread extreme poverty inhibits the full and effective enjoyment of human rights and, in some situations, might constitute a threat to the right to life. Deeply concerned that extreme poverty continues to spread in all countries of the world, regardless of their economic, social and cultural situation, and seriously affect the most vulnerable and disadvantaged individuals, families and groups, who are thus hindered in the exercise of their human rights and their fundamental freedoms."

"Recognizing that the elimination of widespread poverty and the full enjoyment of economic, social and cultural rights are interrelated goals, reaffirms that extreme poverty and exclusion from society constitute a violation of human dignity and that urgent national and international action is therefore required to eliminate them." This concludes some vital quotations that I humbly believe are vital for a relevant and practical assessment with regards to the role of the United Nations in the international arena.

As the world engages the twenty-first century and the next millennium, the United Nations Organization under the distinguished leadership of its Secretary General, His Excellency Kofi Annan, must be prepared to meet the many challenges around the globe. The solutions will definitely not be easy. It's a world perception that the United Nations is merely an international lackey for the only remaining super power, The United States of America. This is a very harsh perception, but this is the perceived reality! If the United Nations is to have a meaningful and productive role in present and future world diplomatic relations, it must work with the sincerity of purpose, in word and deed, to change this negative image. In theory, this seems like an easy task, but when your economic survival and well-being depends on your relationship with your economic master, it is very difficult, if not impossible, to pursue an independent path. It is said that the "power of the purse" determines many things in our lives. It determines how we think, how we vote and even who we remain loyal to. This is a fact of life. America's arrogance in international relations has put the United Nations in some very difficult situations. I sincerely believe, however, that the United Nations has the capacity to live out the true meaning of its creed, despite the many trials that it faces. The world is changing rapidly and domination and supremacy are coming to an end. This is a "Divine Time." The United Nations must now respond to this Divine Time. Even the small and poor nations, despite other economic, or technological incapacity, are refusing to bow to the pressure from the rich and powerful nations. There is a new consciousness today that must be recognized.

The "Power of the Purse" is indeed great, but the "Power of the Creator" is much greater. There are practical economic considerations that the United Nations must face, but they must now fearlessly use and fulfill the great mission of restoring the dignity of humanity. When one reflects on the charter of the Untied Nations, one can see the embodiment of Divine Justice. The challenge now, for this organization, is to inspire its own philosophy.

The role of the United States in international relations is a very simple one. The United States must first move towards being a just nation to its own citizens. They cannot be the moral judge of the world when there is so much injustice in their own backyard. Malcolm X positively espoused: "A man or system which oppresses a man because of his colour is not moral." A race of people is like an individual man, and until it uses its own talent, takes pride in its own history, expresses its own culture, affirms its own selfhood, can never fulfill itself.

"Our history and culture were completely destroyed when we were forcibly brought to America in chains. Now it is important for us to know that our history did not begin with slavery scars. We came from Africa, a great continent and a proud and valued people. A land which is the new world and was the cradle

50

of civilization. Our culture and our history are as old as man itself. Yet, we know almost nothing of it. We must recapture our heritage and our identity if we are ever to liberate ourselves from the bonds of white supremacy. We must launch a cultural revolution to emancipate an entire people."

The constitution of the United States of America, and the Bill of Rights are principles, that if put into practice, can represent the essence of mankind's hopes and good intentions. The American Constitution for all its citizens is a philosophy of Divine Justice. They have deviated from this philosophy because of their lust for power and domination. This attitude must now change if the United States of America is to live out the true meaning of its creed, life, liberty and the pursuit of happiness for all of its citizens, regardless of race, creed or religious oppression. This spirit should also transcend to the international community, a lasting world peace and true prosperity if it is ever to be realized for the human family. This is the challenge for America! The Spirit of Humanity should be initiated in both its domestic and foreign policy initiatives. The evil legacy of supremacy and world domination must be discarded for the well-being of humankind. The United States should also be more consistent in international affairs. The double standard approach should be abandoned. The philosophy of Divine Justice cannot prosper in a climate of arrogance and deception.

It would be most apposite to include what was a very moving experience that exemplifies the spirit and the ideals of universal brotherhood, love and Divine Justice. On Sunday, May 18, 1997 at the historic Malcolm Shabazz Mosque in Harlem, New York City, Ms. Chiara Lubich, the Founder and President of the Focolare Movement which has over 4 million supporters in more than 180 nations, joined in a divine celebration with Imam Warith D. Mohammed, leader of the largest group of Muslims in North America. Imam Warith D. Mohammed is also the Muslim-American spokesman for Human Salvation.

The theme of this epoch making event was "Al-Islam: Unity, Diversity and Inclusion." This was the greatest show of mutual tolerance, enlightened diplomacy and global harmony that I have ever experienced in my lifetime. People from all over the United States, Canada and Europe and all ethnicities lined the streets of Harlem, New York, with mutual anticipation for this memorable occasion. Imams from across the country and region, mingled with priests and nuns and other civic leaders and lay persons. The press organizations, from as far away as the Vatican and other parts of Italy competed for positions with Fox News, Associated Press, Muslim journalists and reporters from the African-American press. Ms. Chiara Lubich, speaking in Italian with simultaneous translation, spoke eloquently of her early days and of the Focolare Movement. She spoke of unity of all people with God and one another as being the core of the Focolare Movement.

She talked about Focolare's goal of bringing into the world the peace that represents unity. "Today's world is longing for unity," she said. "People and countries are trying to come together. In Islam, we see that strong move toward unity as witnessed by the World Muslim League and the World Muslim Congress. One also has seen unity in the World Council of Churches." Chiara Lubich continued by addressing the need for concern for our fellowmen: "We must put it to practice the love of our neighbour. Love your neighbour as yourself. Have your neighbour is right beside you; it matters not who that person is and that neighbour right beside you."

Ms. Lubich expressed that the Christian Golden Rule and the Islamic tradition are the same. She repeated Prophet Muhammad's saying (SAW). "You should want for your brother, what you want for yourself." She noted that there were affinity of the two religions, noting that from her first contact with Islam, she found similarities. "In the great world of Islam there is one God, compassionate and merciful. There is total dedication to God of Will. There is profound faith in love of God." Quoting from the *Holy Qur'an*, she continued. "Allah is closer to us than our jugular veins." She concluded by stating that the event had accomplished a great deal of good, and gave this parting advice: "Go forward with trust and hope working together." After this moving address, Muslim American leader, Imam Warith Mohammed opened by greeting the thousands of Christians, Muslims and others in attendance with *"As-Salaam Alaikum,* peace be unto you."

"We praise God; we witness that God is one who cares about all of His creation especially human creation, we witness that Muhammad is the Seal of the Prophet—the last of the Prophets and Allah's Messenger—God's Messenger." The Imam ended his opening with a salutation to Prophet Muhammad: "Upon him be peace and what follows of that traditional sayings or salute to our Prophet—Ameen."

Referring to the addresses and leadership of Chiara Lubich, Imam Mohammed said: "We are very happy and pleased and feeling our hearts have been blessed to be here to witness the address to this gathering here in Harlem, in the United States of America, by a very special creation of God, this great leader of the Focolare people who is now leading also members of different religions—not only the Catholic community and the Christian community." Imam Mohammed explained how he became acquainted with the true teachings of Islam through the study of the *Holy Qur'an.* That he grew to realize that it is bad not to appreciate the good in other people, regardless of race, nationality, religion, etc. "I finally saw that it wasn't good for us not to embrace the good, appreciate the good, and support the good that we find in others." Imam Mohammed continued: "Whether they belong to the religion or not, whether they are of your colour or not, whether they are of your nationality or not, if you have an opportunity, even support that good, encourage that good and support that good." He concluded by extending the hand of true friendship and brotherhood by working side-by-side together for a better future for all humanity. He cautioned those who desired power or dominance in the world.

The Imam related God's warning to humanity: God said, ***"Whoever wants power or dominance, He will deny it to them! Whoever desires corruption or a dominance,***

they will be denied that by God."

Imam Warith D. Mohammed recently on a National Discussion spoke on Race and Reconciliation. Speaking on behalf of 2.5 million American Muslim constituency, he commented, "I think the issue of race is a serious problem, but I think the more we address it as such, the more we make a big problem of it. Race is a charged word. I think we should discharge it. Many people dress themselves up in race and racism. I think we should want to understand race in its history. Man has an inherent need to feel good about himself as a group. Race is a group. We have to feel good about ourselves as races. All of us are entitled to that. All of us have that demand in our nature to want to feel good about our group. I think blacks need to respect that in themselves and they need to respect that in others. The same for whites." Imam Mohammed on a recent visit to Malaysia also stated: "Islam, though it started in Arabia with the Arabs, was never intended to be just an Arab religion, or the religion of one culture. It is my understanding that, The Holy Prophet Muhammad (SAW), insisted that those who were preachers, who went from him to other parts of the world did understand the culture of the people, but they went to introduce Islam and let Islam do the work of feeding their culture and supporting whatever is excellent, they already had in their culture. Now when I look around the world, I still see a beautiful culture we have on this earth, and that's the way Islam should be.

None of us should be so hung up on our particular race, or nationality, or our culture that we don't see Islam's foundation for human beings is really the humanity. Islam's foundation is upon the humanity of man."

I am indeed very inspired by the righteous, progressive and responsible leadership of Imam Warith D. Mohammed and his divine vision for a united America and a better world for the entire human family.

Imam W. Deen Mohammed is the foremost leader of Muslims throughout America and in many other parts of the world. He is known for his depth of thinking, insight and faith. His perspectives are clearly Qur'anic based, with applications that cut across religious, political, cultural and ethnic lines. He is at the very forefront of interfaith dialogue and cooperation. He is leading the call toward human excellence, refinement and salvation.

Nation of Islam Leader, The Honourable Minister Louis Farrakhan has made several international appeals for Divine Justice, not only for people of colour, but for all people.

The Million Man March was not about hatred for Caucasian or Jewish people, nor was it about black supremacy; rather it was a righteous call for world atonement, world Divine Justice and male personal responsibility and their spiritual, moral and economic duty as husbands and as fathers. Although Minister Farrakhan's message was primarily to African-America men, it positively transcended beyond the shores of North America.

Testimony to this, was shown in Kingston, Jamaica, on June, 16, 1996 on Father's Day at the National Arena, where thousands of jubilant men and women joyfully celebrated the theme of this historic event, which was entitled: "Out Of Many.......One Love."

Pope John Paul II has called for a united world as "The great expectation of today's humanity, the great challenge of our future."

The signs are clear; we are living in a new time in history. If the philosophy and practice of Divine Justice is ever to become a reality on earth, it will definitely begin with visionary human beings such as these, who exemplify this type of righteous and courageous leadership.

I have a special message for former President of the United States of America, William Jefferson Clinton (Bill). The real enemies of these United States, Sir, is not the Libyan people, it is not the Iranian people, it is not the Iraqi people, it is not the Sudanese people, it is not President Fidel Castro or the Cuban people, it is not Islam, the real enemy of America, Sir, is Satan.

Satanic influences have permeated and corrupted both the spiritual and moral fibre of the great nation of the United States of America. Just take a good look at many television screens around the world, just listen to many of the pop songs, just look at the way many people are dressed in public, just take a good look at many streets around the world, just look at the flagrant disrespect for the children and elderly around the globe, just look at what is happening to suffering humanity. It is with sincere hope that you will see more clearly, who is the real enemy of the United States of America, Mr. President, Sir. Could it be the invisible and unseen devil? Thank you.

On Wednesday, June 4, 1997, I had both the honour and the distinction of meeting once again with my beloved brother Kwame Touré, now deceased, known to many as Stokely Carmichael, the conceptualizer of "Ready for Revolution." He was a rare gem of a human being, who is indeed a legend for all time. At this meeting, he sent the following message for the people of Jamaica.

"Sisters and brothers born in Jamaica, I hope these few words find you in the best of health and African Revolutionary spirit. I wish to greet you in the name of our common bond Mother Africa. Enemies would like to let you think you are 'Motherless Children'. But you know your people did not originate in Jamaica. You know your people originated with civilization.

In fact, any African born in Jamaica who thinks that he or she is not African is like an ant in history. They began their origins in slavery because any African who begins his history in Jamaica, began in slavery. They leave out hundreds of thousands of years of civilization in Africa. Those of us who know we are Africans born in Jamaica know of Africa's great contribution to humanity and, therefore, no inferiority complex can be imposed on us by racist terrorism.

We know our people were great in the past and we have a responsibility to restore them to a greater place in the future. Daughters and sons of Africa in Jamaica, it's time to come forward to pick up the banner of African Nationalism and fulfill the dreams of our Pan-African hero, The Honourable Marcus Mosiah Garvey. We must wage revolution for a Unified Socialist Africa that will be strong enough to protect her daughters and sons even in Jamaica. We are always ready for revolution. Your brother in this continued struggle, Kwame Touré."

This profound message will no doubt inspire a timeless legacy. It is with great hope that Jamaica will one day become a truly liberated country and live the true Islamic Spirit of Divine Justice.

My beloved brothers and sisters of Islam, fellow citizens of planet Earth, let us all assiduously strive for the coming of a "New Africa" and a "New World," by positively inculcating the noble Islamic ideal of Divine Justice. We must wage a righteous war that will promote, protect and preserve the dignity of all mankind."

Arnold Toynbee, perhaps the most popular and most respected historian for the West, pays great tribute to Islam in this report of history. "What happened to this Islamic society that was so successful for centuries? They lost what we are trying to get right now. They got too busy with the world and lost Allah and consequently lost the world." Beloved Muslims, we must rekindle the true spirit of Al-Islam. We have two perfect examples, our Holy Book the *Qur'an* and the exemplary life of our beloved Prophet Muhammad (SAW).

Prophet Muhammad was a man building friendships. Christians, Muslims and Jews and people of all religious persuasions need to desire to work for the common good. We can put down the swords of the Crusades and look at Muhammad. We see a man working on building alliances. We see a man committed to human decency, Divine Justice and universal peace. Even with the idolaters who were his enemies, the Prophet made treaties. They often broke them, but still the Prophet made treaties with them. He was a rational man. Many of us would call our Imam infidel or "Kafir" for he would go to a known enemy of Islam to negotiate for better circumstances. But the Prophet did that! Beloved Muslims, we have the right examples. Let us now practically live that right example in word and deed. In closing, I would like to impart a divine thought from the *Holy Qur'an* and an anecdote. This divine message is to world leaders, politicians around the world, leaders of thought, religious leaders, diplomats, scientists, visionaries, business persons and concerned citizens for the salvation of humanity. It reads:

1. *By the Token of Time (through the Ages),*

2. *Verily Man (Humanity) is in loss,*

3. *Except such as have faith, And do righteous deeds, And (join together) In the mutual teaching Of Truth, and of Patience and Constancy.*

Holy Qur'an 103, Surah Al-Asr.

We must all cooperate for the advancement of truth. We also should diligently strive to uphold righteousness with self discipline, perseverance and patience. As world citizens, we all have a vested interest in the improvement and the elevation of humanity. Man's material appetite and existence has to be carefully balanced with the principles of spiritual and moral courage. The traps of extremism should always be avoided in personal, national or international decision making and policy initiatives.

The following anecdote illustrates the inherent oneness of the human race. Many years ago, during the evil Apartheid regime, a Jamaican man of African descent travelled to South Africa. Upon arrival at the airport, he was promptly asked by immigration officials, "Sir would you kindly state to what race you belong?" He responded with the utmost conviction, humour, wit and in the true Jamaican revolutionary spirit, "I would have you gentlemen know that I am a proud and honourable member of the human race." "Can you likewise, say the same?"

An African man, who was the embodiment of a living saint, emphatically expressed to me: "Imam Ali, if you want to kill a man, kill his dreams."

This scourge of "injustice" however subtle must be eradicated from our world.

The message, the solution, and the dream will always be Divine Justice for the universal brotherhood of man. *As-Salaamu-Alaikum* (Peace Be Unto You).

A Perspective from the Author

It is most appropriate to pay a poetic tribute in memory of the innocent victims of the unfortunate and horrific tragedy of September 11th, 2001.

Voices of Unity

Even though there will always be pain,
Those innocent lives were not lost in vain,
To them belong the true victory, the power and the glory.

Why? Why? Why?
There may never be a final goodbye,
All this hating in the world is wrong,
Unity-for everyone,
Never again - 9/11.
Freedom, justice, liberty,
God's way for humanity.

By: Ambassador Imam Douglas Owen-Ali
September 11th, 2002
Kingston, Jamaica

BISMILLAHI ARRAHMAN ARRAHIM.
(In the Name of God, The Compassionate, The Merciful).
AS SALAAM ALAIKUM.
(Peace be unto you).

Beloved Family, Building Bridges of Understanding, Humanity and Hope is indeed a life long journey of faith.

As I endeavor to write on what may be considered a timely and complex topic, it would be appropriate for me to speak openly on my own conversion to Islam, my continued evolution in Islam and my current role as the Islamic Ambassador for Jamaica and the Caribbean Region. As the Representative of the Universal Islamic Centre of America, I have been mandated to serve as the International Ambassador of Peace and an Imam of change.

I was born in both a Christian country and a Christian family. Both my parents were of the Anglican denomination and I also grew up as an Anglican attending the well-known Kingston Parish Church in Jamaica. Therefore, my early upbringing was guided with spiritual, moral and cultural Christian values, attitudes and beliefs. To this day, I can proudly say that the strong character instilled in me at a young age as it relates to the purity of Christianity have co-existed naturally without conflict with my strong Islamic beliefs and traditions. Why is this so? The essence of all religions whether it maybe Christianity, Islam, Judaism, Hinduism, Buddhism, Rastafarian or any religious faith is to bring us as human beings closer to the Almighty Creator and to truly understand the meaning of Divine Love. Thus, the true purpose of any religious faith or doctrine is to acknowledge our common humanity on this planet earth. Rituals may be different, but our path should be one. We should all strive to embrace the path of universal love, humanity and hope.

Twenty-eight years ago, at the tender age of seventeen while attending Miami Dade Community College in Miami Florida, I was persuaded by members of the Nation of Islam to attend Mosque Number twenty nine. I experienced a sensational lecture by the then World Heavyweight Boxing Champion,

Muhammad Ali (The Greatest of all time). He was certainly "floating like a butterfly and stinging like a bee." The Honorable Minister Louis Farrakhan, who was the then National Representative of the Honorable Elijah Muhammad, also brought his fiery spirit of articulation to the event. These two personalities, combined I must say, left me no choice but to embrace the religion of Islam. Their messages were both timely and relevant. As I reflect, there were some things that I did not truly understand, but as a young man searching for identity, and purpose, Islam seemed to be the way. It was the seventies, a time of social change, black consciousness, black identity, the African experience and what one could call a New World Revolution. There was racial tension and hostility in The United States, the opposition to the Vietnam War and a changing world philosophy had emerged.

In Jamaica, at that time the Reggae Revolution and Bob Marley and the Wailers was catching fire around the world. The infectious lyrics and rhythms of Reggae Music along with the Natty Dread Locks created a new consciousness, not only in Jamaica but began to permeate across the Globe. Many of my friends embraced the Rastafarian Faith with pride in their dreadlocks hairstyle, as Bob Marley emerged as a musical and cultural icon. I was given the name of Douglas 3X a "Black Muslim", member of The Nation of Islam and a proud follower of The Honorable Elijah Muhammad. I wore my bald and clean shaved head with pride. The new discipline and culture that I embraced made me say with utmost respect when addressing my brothers in faith and members of the public "yes sir" and "no sir". To this day, this discipline has become part of my character. This spirit of discipline, good manners and decency should be inculcated in the values and attitudes of young people in Jamaica, The United States and communities around the world. The Honorable Elijah Muhammad, the Founder of the Nation of Islam in America and his followers, were known as the infamous "Black Muslims". I, however, even in my spiritual infancy never referred to myself as a "Black Muslim".

Coming from a Jamaican experience, however, which is a multi-racial society, I did not truly understand the term "Black Muslim". I sometimes asked myself why it had to be black. This early experience in The Nation of Islam gave me self-esteem, racial pride, self-discipline and a strong awareness of the importance of moral conduct, coupled with a spirit of brotherly love. This was my initial foundation in Islam and has guided me to this very day. My conversion to Islam at that time was indeed a radical one, but was based on an informed choice. I found a new path to my spiritual, cultural and intellectual existence, but this new path in no way contradicted my strong Christian upbringing in Jamaica. In reflection, it instilled in me a spirit of tolerance and mutual acceptance. This experience, I would say, is no doubt a journey of faith and has prepared me well for a career in international relations and diplomacy. As a spiritual leader, it has also increased my divine understanding as to the importance of dialogue and enlightened tolerance. I am as comfortable in a church or a synagogue or a temple as I am in the Mosque.

Many of my dearest friends are Christians or Jews, some are Black, some are White, some are Chinese, some are Arabs and some are Rastafarians. "Colour is not the problem, it is the heart and mind of man." My evolution to Islam has come with time. Some of it came while pursuing post graduate studies in International Law and Diplomacy at the University of Lagos in Nigeria, West Africa. My continued evolution in Islam is still in process and can be compared to that of the great Malcolm X. Islam is not about being an Arab, it is not about being Black, it is not about being White, it is not about being Indian, it is not about being Asian, it is all about the humanity of man. We serve one God on the path to divine universal love for the entire human family. May Almighty Allah (God) increase us with the spirit of divine understanding. No more artificial barriers, no more boundaries, no more global intolerance, no more hatred and divisiveness a vision of a world where we will one day all enjoy "justice for every race, equality in every place."

Ambassador
Imam Douglas Owen-Ali

Building in Action

The Jamaican Connection

"Imam Ali meets The Prime Minister"

▲ *The Imam visiting Jamaica House.*

▲

◄ *Imam Ali makes presentations to Prime Minister of Jamaica, the Most Honourable Percival James Patterson, on his visit to Jamaica House after returning from his studies in Nigeria.*

▲ *"The Imam meets The Leader of the Opposition"*
*Presenting a copy of The Holy Qur'an to the Leader of the
Opposition in Jamaica, the Most Honourable Edward Seaga.*

▲ *Imam Ali presenting his
credentials to the Governor
General of Jamaica Sir Howard
Cooke. Looking on is the Public
Defender of Jamaica, Mr.
Howard Hamilton, Q.C.*

◄

*Imam Ali visiting Minister Portia
Simpson-Miller on the occasion of
her birthday at her office in
Kingston.*

Building Bridges
between Jamaica and the USA

Ambassador Ali and friends presenting a gift of flowers to US Ambassador to Jamaica, Her Excellency Sue Cobb in 2003.

Ambassador Ali and publisher Mike Henry, ▲ presenting the cover of the new book (Islam Building Bridges of Understanding) to US Ambassador to Jamaica, Her Excellency Sue Cobb.

(c) The Gleaner Co. Ltd

▲ *Imam Ali meets Her Excellency Sue Cobb, United States Ambassador to Jamaica and her husband at prayer service at Stella Maris Church in Kingston in September 2001.*

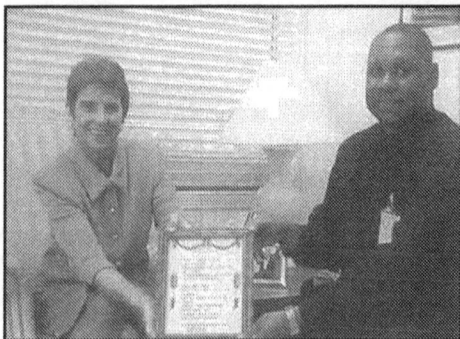

Imam Ali presenting a gift of his poem "Voices of ▲ Unity" to Her Excellency Ambassador Sue Cobb, United States Ambassador to Jamaica.

Imam Ali & Minister Louis Farrakhan

▶

Presenting the give of a Kufi to the Honourable Minister Louis Farrakhan which he wore on his historic visit to the Jewish Synagogue in Jamaica in March 2002.

A spirit of brotherly embrace: ▲
From L-R: Mr. Howard Hamilton, Q.C., Public Defender of Jamaica; Imam Douglas Owen-Ali; Honourable Minister Louis Farrakhan; businessman, Mr. Ransford White and Mr. Junior Lincoln, chief organizer of the

▲ **The Spirit of friendship:** *The Imam presents a gift of a Kufi to Mr. Joshua Farrakhan, son of the Minister.*

◀

Imam Douglas Owen-Ali presenting a copy of the first edition of his book to the Honourable Minister Louis Farrakhan at a dinner reception in Kingston, Jamaica in March 2002. Looking on are Professor Trevor Monrose and others who attended the ceremony.

The Honourable Minister Louis Farrakhan, Leader of the Nation of Islam meets Chairman and Managing Director of The Gleaner Company Limited, Mr. Oliver Clarke, at a luncheon hosted by Mr. Clarke in Kingston in March 2002. Looking on are Members of the business community in Jamaica.

The Honourable Louis Farrakhan greets Mrs. Pauline Owen, the mother of Ambassador Imam Douglas Ali. In background (From right) are Mr. Mike Henry, Mrs. Glynne Manley and Mr. Joseph Manley.

"A Moment in History". ▲
The Hon Minister Louis Farrakhan, Leader of the National Islam, makes a historic visit to the Jewish Synagogue in Kingston, Jamaica in March 2002. The Synagogue was originally built in 1885, but was partially destroyed in the 1907 earthquake. The building was restored in 1912 and is the only remaining synagogue in Jamaica. To his left are Mr. Ainsley Henriques, Local Jewish Leader, and Ambassador Imam Douglas Owen Ali, the International Ambassador of Peace for Jamaica and the Caribbean.

Visiting and Discussing Building Bridges

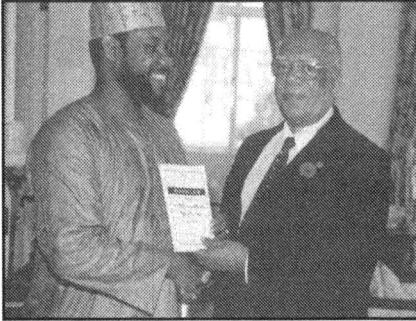

▲ *Imam Ali presenting a copy of his book to the Governor General of Jamaica Sir Howard Cooke.*

▲ *Former Jamaican Ambassador and Elder Statesman Keith Johnson, OJ; meets Professor Gambari along with Her Excellency Patricia Durrant, Jamaica's Permanent Representative to the United Nations, in New York in 1998.*

▲ *Imam Ali presenting a copy of his book to visiting Head of Iranian Trade Delegation to Jamaica.*

▲ *Professor Gambari making a point during his speech at the book launching ceremony in New York in 1998, looking on is Nigeria's Consul General to the United States.*

▲ *Imam Ali meets His Excellency Muhamed Sacribey, Ambassador / Permanent Representative of Bosnia to the United Nations in New York in 1998.*

◀

"Jamaican Connection"
Imam presenting copy of his book to reggae singer Abijah at United States Embassy during Black History Month Lecture.

Imam Ali presenting a gift to His Excellency Professor Ibrahim Gambari and Mr. Ismail Shamsid-deen of Development Outreach Inc., in New York.

▶

◀

Imam Ali presenting a copy of his book to the Dean of the Diplomatic Corp. in Jamaica, His Excellency Fernando Pardo Huerta, Ambassador of Chile to Jamaica.

▶

Ambassador Keith Johnson in discussion with the Imam at the book launching ceremony, in New York in 1998.

▶

Imam Ali presenting a copy of his book to Jamaican Minister of Government Dr. the Honourable Paul Robertson.

◀

Imam Ali presenting a copy of his book to Ambassador G. Anthony Hylton at a private reception.

▶

Imam Ali presenting a copy of his earlier book to His Excellency Professor Ibrahim Gambari, Nigeria's Ambassador/ Permanent Representative to the United Nations, in New York in 1998.

◀

Imam Ali accepts the Humanitarian Award from Islamic leader in New York at book launching ceremony in 1998. Looking on is his mother (right) and former wife (left).

Economic Initiatives of Ambassador Imam Douglas Owen-Ali

◄

In discussions with Honourable Minister of Commerce and Technology Phillip Paulwell and Mustafa Abdul-Hakim Dyer, International Investment Banker and Consultant at a private reception.

Imam Ali and Publisher, Mr. Mike Henry, at Gulf Investment Initiative press conference in New York in 2001. ►

◄

Imam Ali presenting copy of his earlier book to Nigerian High Commission to Jamaica, Her Excellency Mrs. Florentina Adenike Ukonga.

►

Imam Ali greets former Nigerian High Commissioner to Jamaica His Excellency Professor Emmanuel Ugochukwu at the Nigerian High Commission in Kingston.

◄

Imam Ali in discussions with Publisher Mr. L. Michael Henry, CD, MP and Dr. Oswald Harding OJ, QC, at press conference in Kingston.

▶

Imam Ali and family at press conference in Kingston in 2001.

◄

Imam Ali presenting a copy of his book to Deputy Sudanese Ambassador to the United Nations Mubarak Hussein Rahmtalla in New York in 2001. Looking on is Mr. Archibald Hammond, of Global Oneness Limited.

▶

Imam Ali meets a member of the Rastafarian Community at a Press Conference in Kingston, Jamaica.

Page 6 THE DAILY OBSERVER Monday, February 18, 2002

❿EWS

www.jamaicaobserver.com

Bloody Sunday, a documentary-style account of the 1972 killing of civil rights activists in northern Ireland by British soldiers, and the Japanese animated feature Spirited Away shared the top prize at the Berlin film festival yesterday — Page 17

Local Muslim leader lobbying rich Arab states for US$100m

BY VERNON DAVIDSON
Senior Associate Editor

ONE of the leaders of Jamaica's Muslim community is seeking US$100 million over five years from rich Arab states to build an Islamic cultural centre in Kingston that, he said, will provide a range of services to Muslims and non-Muslims.

According to Imam Douglas Owen-Ali, the Islamic Cultural Centre of Jamaica is intended to be a satellite of Islamic values that will be so involved in the Jamaican way of life that it will be viewed as a culture within a culture.

"We have developed a five-year business plan," Owen-Ali told the *Observer* in a recent interview. "I'm going, in a few weeks, to meet with some Arab ambassadors in New York and Washington and I'm saying there are some things that I need. I will be talking to the moderate Gulf states — Saudia Arabia, Kuwait and the United Arab Emirates."

According to Owen-Ali, the Islamic cultural centre will comprise a national mosque, an Islamic educational centre, Islamic research and communication centre, lecture theatre conference centre, a life centre which would include a nursery, day-care centre, wellness centre, restaurant, bakery and meat market catering to the ethnic tastes of Muslims, a zakat (charity) house and a facility that will provide financial and business advice, as well as funding for projects.

"We would like to have Islamic banks that provide non-interest loans and offer profit-sharing," explained Owen-Ali, who said that that concept is now being adopted in Europe.

He also wants to build an Islamic hospital "for all people", a development that would help enable him realise a part of his greater plan to increase the Muslim population in Jamaica from the current 11,000 to at least 50,000 in the next five years.

Owen-Ali, who was last September named by the Universal Islamic Centre of America as their ambassador to Jamaica and the Caribbean, is convinced that to have that many Jamaicans become Muslims, he needs to offer something tangible.

"I am a friend of the underprivileged poor," he said, "I am a shepherd of the less fortunate. But to minister to these lost souls, I need to bring tangible things to the table."

He believes that while man cannot live by bread alone, man cannot live without bread. Therefore, he intends to ensure that he has the financial backing to set up and sustain the kinds of programmes that will improve the lives of Jamaicans in need.

"We need sustainable programmes in communities," he argued. "We have problems in the inner-cities of this country... how do we provide jobs, self-help programmes, education. You cannot go to somebody in this day and tell them come pray five times a day and read the *Qur'an*. You have to come first and give them tangible things.

"So, I will be seeking financial support to empower me to be an effective ambassador to Jamaica and the Caribbean."

Owen-Ali said he was approached with the offer to become an envoy at an Islamic conference in Chicago last August, attended by Muslims from about 35 countries.

"Allah has blessed me with a gift to speak," said Owen-Ali. "I had delivered a moving speech, after which the Sheikh from Ghana came to me and said 'brother, we have to encourage you. Imam, I'd like to you to be our ambassador'. That is how it emerged. Not because I'm any great scholar or great spiritual guru, but Allah has blessed me with the ability to move people and I've qualified myself by my own academic work."

Owen-Ali holds his first degree in marketing and a Masters degree in International Law and Diplomacy from the University of Lagos in Nigeria.

He has written two books, the first, titled *Islamic Law and International Relations*, was launched in Kano state, Nigeria. Now, he said, he's writing his third.

"I'm doing things. I'm a show me person. Tell me that you can recite the *Qur'an* all day long and you can't show me what you're doing has no meaning," he said.

His instrument of authority, he said, mandates him as ambassador to accomplish the Universal Islamic Centre of America's vision to not only build mosques and Islamic centres, but to "facilitate the increasing demands people from all over the world by teaching the knowledge and love of Allah".

In order to fulfil that mandate, said Owen-Ali, he needs to establish a national mosque, an Islamic school, in Jamaica.

That mosque, he said, would be striking, easily recognised unlike the one on Red Hills Road where most of the city's Muslims worship. "Something that represents the dignity of Islam. We need a monument to represent Islam and to attract Christians to our way of life.

"My mother keeps telling me 'son, a so-called mosque at Red Hills Road is not going to make it'. My colleagues, who are university graduates, they want to come to something that is dignified."

Owen-Ali is also adamant that in order to pull more people to his religion, he and the Muslim community must look at Islam as a product and make it attractive.

"One of the challenges Muslims must face is how to package Islam in a way that will make it attractive to the people of Jamaica and the wider Caribbean," he argued.

"I believe that one of the ways for Islam to impact the people of Jamaica and the wider Caribbean is through commerce. We cannot see Islam in isolation from commerce," he said. "If you're commercially strong, government listens to you."

Muslims, he said, must now work to become a strong lobby, through their 'numbers and through commerce. "We need to have a stronger sense of community. Many of us believe that it is good enough to sit in the mosque. Now we have to take Islam out of the mosque," Owen-Ali said, while advising his Muslim colleagues to play a responsible role in politics.

"Politics is a way of life in Islam. I will say to my colleague Muslims that we must embark on a politics that is righteous and principled."

That, he said, requires them living the ideals of Islam in its purity. "I'm saying to people, we want to give you paradise here on earth and we want paradise for you in the hereafter."

OWEN-ALI... we cannot see Islam in isolation from commerce

Imam Douglas Owen-Ali, right, accepting a copy of Third World's 'Ain't Giving Up,' from Stephen 'Cat' Coore, after announcing plans for a world tour of building bridges between world building bridges between world regions, in the wake of the Iraqi war and the differences between Islam and other religions at the Oasis Restaurant, Hope Gardens, Kingston.

THE GLEANER ● Wednesday, May 2, 2001   BUSINESS   D4

Jamaica businesses offered Islamic links

By Balford Henry
Senior staff reporter

JAMAICAN-BORN Islamic scholar Imam Douglas Owen-Ali thinks it is time the Caribbean took toward Islamic nations for economic co-operation and support.

A professor of the University of Lagos with a mandate to international law and diplomacy and author of the book, ISLAMIC LAW AND INTERNATIONAL RELATIONS, Owen-Ali considers himself the international ambassador for the promotion of Islamic interests in the region.

He says that he intends to bring his professional expertise to bear on the Islamic cause in Jamaica and the wider Caribbean and plans to kick-off his efforts next month in the United States.

Imam Owen-Ali, a devout Muslim and founder/executive chairman of Global Oneness, Inc., will lead a Jamaican mission to New York this month for the launch of the Gulf Investment Initiative(GIII).

The team is expected to include business sector Mynila Blythe and Dr. Franklyn Johnston of Troppy, Johnson and Associates, who will serve as special adviser.

They will target new investment initiatives under the GIII at meetings with Gulf States ambassadors as well as with prominent African-American interest groups like the Caribbean-American Programme for Empowerment(CAPE). The highlight of the visit will be a discussion which will bring together Gulf State ambassadors and representatives of the broader Caribbean-American business community and the Jamaican mis-

...sion, in a bid to develop a bonds of friendship and mutual trust and with a view to forge and cement new investment arrangements between them.

"All United Nations ambassadors from the states involved will be present and there will be opportunities for meaningful contact with influential Gulf ambassadors, which will serve to launch this new initiative," Imam Owen-Ali said.

He said that the purpose of the Jamaican mission is to create commercial relationships between Jamaica/Caribbean businesses and African expatriate and Islamic communities in the United States and the Gulf State.

"We think we can attract significant volume of foreign direct investment to Jamaica and the rest of the Caribbean from the Gulf States, specifically the Gulf Co-operation Council countries which include Saudi Arabia, Kuwait, the United Arab Emirates, Bahrain, Qatar and Oman, as well as the wider Muslim world," he explained. "This will be an initiative, representing a shift in focus that is timely, an idea whose time has come and a solid opportunity, embracing for Jamaica, as it seeks for significant presence in the Muslim states," he added.

The delegation will be hosted/recognised by important Gulf States ambassadors and will seek courtesy calls on some prominent interests at the United Nations.

As a prelude to the mission, former acting president/CEO of the United Bank of Kuwait's Islamic Banking Division, Abdul Hakim Dyer, visited Jamaica last month as a guest of Imam Owen-Ali, to hold exploratory talks with members of the Jamaican private sector.

Imam Owen-Ali said that the project has come to a time when countries, previously divided by various causes, including religious and cultural, find it imperative to come together for mutual business-to-commercial, political and diplomatic base...

"enlightened nationalism concept" underlying the philosophy espoused by His Royal Highness Prince Bandar Bin Sultan Bin Abdul Aziz, ambassador extraordinary and plenipotentiary of the Kingdom of Saudi Arabia to the US. "He believes that commercial interests serve longer than those barriers, when countries do business together," Owen-Ali explained.

But, Owen-Ali says his project is not only about commerce and investment, as his own Global Oneness, Inc. will be positioning to foster, "Investing in The Children of the World," which he says he aims to do by providing a concept of global oneness.

THE DAILY OBSERVER Thursday, July 13, 2000 Page 7

OPINION

Imam Douglas Owen-Ali, friend of the unbefriended poor

BY
MARK
WIGNALL

IN September 1998 when I obtained a copy of the book Islamic Law and International Relations written by Imam Douglas Owen-Ali, I read it and made my usual privately written comments. Although I thought the book had a lot to offer in the way of giving to the world a new perspective to international relations and jurisprudence, the very fact that it was written by an Imam, a Muslim spiritual leader, made me hold back on making public comments on the publication.

Of course, it had nothing to do with the book being written either from a Muslim, a Christian or a Jewish perspective. It had more to do with me not being a religious person.

But just a few weeks ago, a matter was brought to my attention and the name Imam Douglas Owen-Ali came up again. Although he was reluctant to give full details of the matter when we spoke last weekend, I have gathered enough of the man and his mission to give my readers a perspective which I believe they will find interesting.

The Imam (spiritual leader) is a 43-year-old Jamaican who has been a muslim for the past 25 years. He is a man with a mission. According to the Imam, his present and lifetime mission is, "To forge a strategic, spiritual, economic, diplomatic, political and cultural alliance with the Muslim world that will redound to the benefit of humanity."

One morning a few weeks ago the Imam got up to do the first of his five daily prayers (FAJR). At about that time, First News on TVJ carried an item that affected him greatly. The news was about young 15-month-old Shanice Wright of Greenvale in Manchester who was diagnosed with a diseased liver.

The national appeal was for a sound liver to save the life of the young, innocent infant. According to Imam Owen-Ali, "Spiritually, I responded. What this meant is that I had made a commitment in, and from, my heart to give the

...youngster the assistance which was needed."

When I enquired of him as to the rush to commit himself without having the ready means to do so, he explained to me that it was not an option among Muslims to help the less unfortunate. "The third pillar of Islam is charity which is a form of self-taxation for distribution to the poor. In the Muslim world it is known as "zakkat."

"Within half an hour, I received a call from Washington and from there it was converted to a country in the Middle East. The Imam was uncomfortable with giving me the name of the country so I asked him not to publish it.

As we explained, it is the story of a child to give charity but it is not to be headed about loudly. In giving me the information, he further explained that in a large Christian country such as Jamaica, any assistance from the Muslim community that could be borne so beneficially as the works of charity being carried out by the Christian community ought to be considered worthy of some publicity, especially when the differences in the outlook of both religions are misunderstood on both sides.

Any reasonable method that could be seen to be helping to bridge the religious gap must be utilised.

The assistance from the Middle Eastern country will be coming in the next few days, I am informed.

The Imam studied in Nigeria and obtained his Masters' degree in International Law and Diplomacy from the University of Lagos Faculty of Law in Nigeria in 1995. As a Muslim scholar and a Jamaican he is deeply concerned that even in the all-compelling push to globalisation, the world seems to be moving apart rather than coming together out of a real wish to fulfil the needs of its peoples.

In a quote from his book, Islamic Law and International Relations, he states, "Development becomes a goal-and-value-oriented activity, devoted to the optimisation of human well-being in all these dimensions. The moral and material, the economic, political and the social, the spiritual and the physical are inseparable."

The book further states that "... mankind has a common destiny aimed at the attainment of the noble ideals of justice, peace, unity, equity, brotherhood and international love. If the proposed New World Order is to have any meaningful impact for mankind's future humanity, it must be guided by these items".

As we speak on his surprisingly cool verandah in the heat of the Jamaican summer, I sense that the Imam is a man with a mission. I explain to him that I have read his book but I am also seeking his broader objectives and where Jamaica fits into his mission. He tells me.

Imam Douglas Owen-Ali believes that the time has now come when countries that were previously apart must now come together for mutual political, diplomatic and commercial

benefits. He believes that Jamaica should now position itself as part of this global challenge. It is in this light, he believes, that the entire Muslim world should now be targeted as part of our global economic alliance.

He tells me that a wise man once said that "... the fortunate is the one who spends and gives away; the unfortunate is the one who dies and leaves behind."

Too many of our Jamaican people are trying to be like each other, to be a part of the herd and willing to commit to the dictates of the wild herd. Imam Owen-Ali is not from that mould and one senses that he is about to tackle the world if that is what it will take to attain his mission of global peace and justice.

He quotes the Q'uran, Sura 63 Ayat 10, "And spend out of what we have given you before death comes to one of you, so that he should say, My Lord! Why didn't you not reprise me to a near term, so that I should have given alms and been of the doers of good deeds."

Little Shanice Wright of Greenvale, Manchester, will soon be given a chance at life, a chance to attain adulthood. The Imam does not see his assistance as anything special; it is just another part of his mission which is global in its scope and economic in its outlook.

He reminds me of a statement made by His Royal Highness Prince Bandar, ambassador of the Kingdom of Saudi Arabia to the United States: "Commercial interests survive longer than strategic interests. When countries do business together, they stay together."

The Imam ends the interview with, "God/Allah chooses every human being to fulfil a divine mission on earth. My mission on earth is not merely the accumulation of material possessions, wealth and power, but rather to be a friend of the unbefriended poor, a servant, a keeper and a shepherd to the less fortunate of this world."

I feel a better man as I leave his home and also I feel real good about him being a Jamaican and, at the same time, a universal man with endless possibilities and a boundless store of energy.

Building Bridges for the Future: Youth & Global Oneness

◀

Imam Ali at home with the children from the S.O.S. Children's Village in Stony Hill, Jamaica.

Imam Ali with Children from the Maxfield Park Children's Home at Black History Month lecture in Kingston in 2002. ▼

Global Oneness! (Excerpts)
Giving Hope to Children
at the Maxfield Park Children Home.

As Technology develop and people become more aware, barriers get broken down and people become closer. Colour, class and creed fade into obscurity when we consider the might and power of the Creator and His gift of life, love, and kindness. The world gets smaller on a daily basis and we become one in the face of the Almighty Creator. Ambassador Imam Douglas Owen-Ali Spiritual Leader, author, poet, scholar, humanitarian and International Relations Consultant known to many as the *"friend of the unbefriended poor"* is the Founder and Executive Chairman of the Global Oneness Organization an International Relations consulting firm and humanitarian organization devoted to the uplift of disenfranchised children in Jamaica the Caribbean and around the world.

As the International Ambassador of Peace, his global mission is one of service to humanity and one of building bridges of understanding, humanity and hope for the entire human family. Imam Ali is spearheading the global mission to highlight the plight of children who have been disenfranchised and abandoned, street kids and those placed in children homes. As he seeks to generate support for the development of Care Centers firstly for the children of Jamaica and the Caribbean region with eventual expansion to the Global Village. Ambassador Ali is concerned about the problems faced by innocent children of the world. He believes that his mission on earth would not be complete until facilities were put in place on a global scale to provide shelter, food, education, health services and home care for those neglected by their societies.

Ambassador Ali's passion also includes the empowerment of disenfranchised children universally. As a Goodwill Ambassador for the Maxfield Park children's home he recently sponsored 30 children from the home to attend the Jazz Workshop for Musicians in the making. The United States Embassy in partnership with distinguished Jamaican sponsors organized this workshop, which was held in the School of Music Auditorium at the Edna Manley College of the Visual and Performing Arts, on Arthur Wint Drive in Kingston. The music workshop was put on for Inner city kids as part of a celebration of African American History Month entitled, "CHILLIN" with Melba Joyce and the Maurice Gordon Jazz Quartet.

Ambassador Imam Douglas Owen-Ali who also addressed the gathering at the end of the workshop and spoke of the Global Oneness Mission and Vision to launch the humanitarian mission to help the children of the world. And his plans as an International Relations Consultant in collaboration with enlightened corporate citizens of the world who will join him with this worthy cause. Imam Ali said Global Oneness would seek to identify appropriate sites in Jamaica for the establishment of Care Centers where children will be housed and cared for. These facilities will provide food and shelter, guidance counselors, health care facilities, educational facilities, trade training centers, agriculture training, employment opportunities that will provide sustainable growth and development for the young people of Jamaica.

He said, the immediate needs are health care, as due to the lack of adequate facilities, many young children lay in hospital beds awaiting vital life saving operations with no immediate hope in sight. Homeless children wander about the streets in urban centers as they seek the basic necessities of life, food and shelter. "Children cannot learn when they are hungry" he said, "many leave the classroom to beg for food on the streets."

Orna Blum, Public Affairs Officer at the US Embassy in Kingston expressed satisfaction for the level of participation by the young people. She thanked everyone for coming and she specifically thanked the Global Oneness Family and other enlightened corporate sponsors for the financial and moral support they gave as the Embassy looks forward to doing it again next year. Imam Ali continues to exemplify and embrace the Global Oneness Philosophy, "Embracing the spirit of the Human Family". We look forward to the Building Bridges world tour scheduled to begin in the summer of 2003. His music CD of the same name and his new book, Islam Building Bridges of Understanding, Humanity and Hope will be released internationally and will also be available for the local market. The mission of building bridges is a timely one and we do hope that this message will resonate globally for the benefit of humankind.

MONDAY, APRIL 6, 1987

'Rapatak' and his 'Say No to Drugs' campaign

His mission is a fight against drug abuse among young people and his name is 'Rapatak'.

Enthusiastic and full of zeal, Douglas 'Dougie' Owen has taken on the stage name 'Rapatak' and the 'Say No' to drugs cause from his New York City home, to Kingston.

"I want to tell the young people here that using drugs is a 'no-no' and my style of telling them is unique," he says. He is right.

Dressed in his stage garb and with his taped music, Dougie at first 'raps' with his audience, mainly young people, about the dangers of the use of cocaine, ganja and other drugs. 'Rapping', he explains, is a fast-talking style of American deejaying.

On a brief visit to the **Gleaner** Dougie and his assistant, Kevern King, spoke to us about their 'Say No to Drugs' campaign.

He said that they had been to several schools, including; Seaforth All-Age and Penwood All-Age, where Dougie has performed and then given the young people a talk on the dangers of drug abuse.

"The children really like the rapping and they join in when I'm doing it," he said; and also pointed out that he has plans to release a single on his anti-drug campaign in June this year.

"I tell the kids to get high on life, music and sports instead of on drugs.I encourage them to love

'RAPATAK': Douglas Owen, 'Rapatak'.   Shaw photo

themselves and I tell them about the importance od education.

"I say: Look at me. Yyou think I'm crazy. Well, I am. I'm crazy about life. I use the name 'Rapatak'

as my stage character and when I'm rapping with the kids I do the junkie walk. Which is how the junkies look when they're spaced out ".

His interest in the anti-drugs campaign was aroused when he saw what the abuse of drugs was doing to the lives of young people in New York.

He said that he has already lectured in several schools and colleges on the evils of drug abuse, under the sponsorship of several firms.

Douglas said that he has plans to tour and lecture in 20 to 30 cities in the United States, in schools and communities; and he hopes to get help from Don King and Muhammed Ali in this campaign which he plans to bring to Jamaica when next he visits. He has been here for three months and plans to leave sometime this month.

Born in Kingston, he grew up in the United States. He is a public relations consultant.

— **Yvonne Grinam**

OWEN-ALI

Imam calls for unity

INTERNATIONAL ISLAMIC ambassador of peace for the Caribbean, Imam Douglas Owen-Ali has launched a campaign to "build bridges" between religions in the region, including Islam, Christianity, Judaism and Rastafarianism, as well as other faiths.

Imam Owen-Ali announced plans for his missions which will include a world tour to promote his book **Islam –**

Building Bridges of Understanding, Humanity and Hope, as well as an album of peace-promoting songs written by him and arranged by Shiah Coore, son of Third World band leader, Stephen 'Cat' Coore.

"As an international ambassador of peace, my views reflect the ideals of freedom, justice and liberty, as God's way for humanity: Muslim, Christian, Jew, the Creator made all of you; not to hate, not to separate, but to journey together in the oneness of faith."

He added: "The music reflects the unity and diversity of human kind. In this time of great divisiveness, I seek to bring about the unity of the family."

THE GLEANER ● Monday, September 3, 2001

Islamic leader calls for greater unity

By Balford Henry
Staff Reporter

A CALL for greater unity among Muslims worldwide was made by Jamaican Islamic leader Imam Douglas Owen Ali in Chicago, United States recently.

Imam Ali was among some 50 speakers from across the world at the International Islamic symposium 2001, held at the Ramada Plaza O'Hare, Chicago.

He challenged the entire Muslim world, Arabs as well as non-Arabs, to seek to fulfill "the great legacy of Prophet Muhammad," by seeking to address the urgent needs of its believers and to try to work together for world peace and unity.

Imam Ali urged the Muslim community to support charitable ventures like his Global Oneness Initiative, which is aimed at providing support for poor and disenfranchised children in Jamaica, as well as Gulf Investment Initiative, which is seeking to generate US$500 million in foreign direct investments for Jamaica and other sections of the Caribbean.

He said that Muslims could no longer remain trapped by the confines of tradition. "The time has now come for us in Jamaica and the Caribbean region to broaden our horizons economically, culturally and spiritually to avoid being dominated by what is being termed globalisation," he told the meeting.

He was speaking at the first plenary session of the symposium which had as its theme "The Seerah of Prophet Muhammad in the Light of the New Millennium." The event was hosted by the Universal Islamic Center in conjunction with the Islamic Studies and Research Association and the World Islamic Mission.

The symposium focused on the birth, life and legacy of the last prophet and messenger, Allah Muhammad. Organisers said that it was triggered by the fact that, despite tremendously significant efforts by various religious and spiritual leaders, "the human family is still incapable of preventing or stopping the proliferation of weapons of mass destruction, as well as the perpetuation of very horrible acts of war and complicated conflicts which continue to claim the lives of innocent children, women and people all around the world."

Other speakers included representatives from Bangladesh, Canada, Egypt, England, Ghana, Jordan, Nigeria, Pakistan, Palestine, Panama, Senegal, Sudan, Syria and the United States.

Prior to the meeting, Imam Ali had led a team of Jamaican business people to New York in July for the launch of his charitable Global Oneness organisation, as well as for trade discussions with the Muslim business community. The local team included businessmen Neville Blythe and Junior Lincoln, politicians Mike Henry and Hyacinth Bennett, Dr. Franklyn Johnston and Dr. Lloyd Cole.

Diplomatic Initiatives: Building Bridges of Support

With friends at book launching ceremony at Terra Nova Hotel in Kingston in 1998.

Paying a courtesy call along with other members of the Global Oneness Organization on Mr. William Rodgers Senior President of Air Jamaica Ltd.

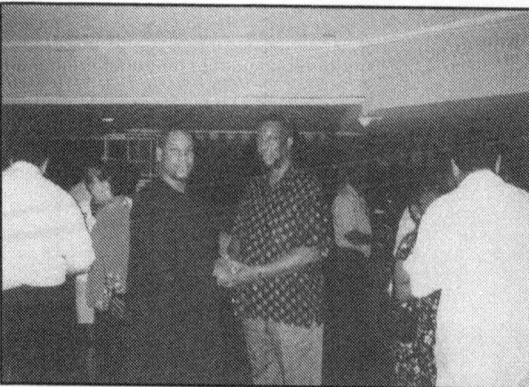

Greeting Dr. James M. Corbett, Deputy Director of Youth Crime Watch of America at a reception in Kingston.

◄

"Building Bridges of Understanding"
*Greeting a Brother from the Kingdom of
Saudi Arabia Al-Zaidi Sulaiman, at the
Hilton Hotel in Kingston in 2002.
Looking on in another Muslim brother
Ronald Waite.*

►

*Welcoming Andrew Cocking
of Capital and Credit
Merchant Bank in Jamaica
To "Jarabian Nite"
Reception.*

◄

**"Meeting The Chief
Justice of Jamaica"**
*Presenting a copy of his earlier
book to the Lord Chief Justice of
Jamaica Lensley Wolfe at The
Supreme Court in Kingston. Also
in attendance are Mr. Howard
Hamilton Q.C. the Public
Defender of Jamaica and other
members of the Global Oneness
Organization.*

September 11th

▶

"Greeting a Special Lady"
Embracing The Honourable
Portia Simpson-Miller, Jamaican
Minister of Government at the
United States Embassy Inter-
Faith Service remembering the
victims of September 11, 2001.
Looking on is Mr. Ronald Waite a
friend of Ambassador Ali.

◀

In discussions with the
Leader of the Opposition
the Most Honourable
Edward Seaga and Dr.
Oswald Harding O.J. at
the United States
Embassy. The Occasion
was a service of Inter-
Faith Unity remembering
the victims of September
11, 2001.

◄

"An Evening of Oneness"
Ambassador Imam Douglas
Owen-Ali entertains Former
Deputy Chief of Mission at
the United States Embassy in
Kingston, Mr. Richard Smyth
and Former United States
Consul General to Jamaica
Mr. Donald Wells.

►

Ambassador Ali greets The
President of the University of
Technology Mr. Rae Davies along
with Dr. Andrew Cocking of
Capital and Credit Merchant
Bank in Jamaica.

"Building Bridges of Understanding, A Historic Moment"
Ambassador Imam Douglas Owen-Ali and Minister Andrew Muhammad,
welcome former Deputy Chief of Mission at the United States Embassy in
Kingston, Mr. Richard Smyth and Mr. Stephen Henriques, Acting Spiritual
Leader of the Jewish Community in Jamaica to Muhammad Mosque in
Kingston. This Historic Event of Building Bridges of Understanding was a
milestone in Muslim-Jewish Relations in Jamaica. The Imam delivered the
Khutbah (Sermon) at The Juma Service to celebrate the occasion.

EMBASSY OF THE
UNITED STATES OF AMERICA
KINGSTON

OFFICE OF THE AMBASSADOR

September 20, 2002

Imam Douglas Owen Ali
Universal Islamic Centre of America
30 Havendale Drive
Kingston 19

Dear Imam Ali:

I would like to thank you for your eloquent contribution to the American Embassy's Remembrance and Unity Candlelight Ceremony on the anniversary of the September 11 attacks. Your involvement in the Interfaith Ceremony Service enabled all of us to focus on the fact that, as a result of the atrocities of September 11, 2001 in the United States, citizens of all countries must remain united in the common goal of maintaining our freedom and human rights. Your meaningful poem added a lovely and unique touch.

All members of the American Embassy community extend their sincere gratitude to you for your willingness to share in this ceremony of remembrance and unity.

Sincerely,

Sue M. Cobb
Ambassador

Unity Candlelight Ceremony on the anniversary of September 11, 2001.

Local Muslims react

JAMAICAN MUSLIM LEADER, IMAM Douglas Owen-Ali, has condemned Tuesday's terrorist action in the United States as an "insane attack on the United States".

In a statement on Friday, Imam Owen-Ali said: "As a practising and devout Muslim and a citizen of the United States of America and one who adheres to the divine injunctions of our beloved holy prophet Muhammad, I utterly condemn this insane attack on the United States of America and its innocent citizens.

"I ask all well-thinking Muslims, Christians, Jews and people of all religious beliefs worldwide, to join me in the condemnation of this evil and despicable acts against humanity. We offer our sincere prayers and condolences to the families and loved ones of the innocent victims.

"We must not allow this unconscionable act of terrorism to jeopardise the attainment of world peace and global oneness. We pray God that those responsible will face the swift wrath of divine justice."

Imam Owen-Ali, head of Global

■ **Owen-Ali**

Oneness, a charitable organization linking Muslims around the world, said that the action has had a negative effect on the Muslim community worldwide, including Jamaica, because of the allegations that it could have been committed by members of the faith.

He said that one example was the fact that a visit to Jamaica by a Saudi Arabian elite for a public address in Kingston next week, has had to be postponed because of the developments surrounding the act of terrorism.

He said that while he did not expect the kind of animosity which is being shown to certain Muslim communities in the United States since the incident to be replicated in Jamaica, he was concerned that Jamaicans could see Islam in a distorted light.

30 HAVENDALE DRIVE
KINGSTON 19
JAMAICA WI.
TEL:(876)925-1092
FAX:(876)926-6147
email:malcom@ruthvenlaw.com

email: malcolm@ruthvenlaw.com

ember 27, 2001

Mr. George W. Bush
President
United States of America
White House
1600 Pennsylvania Avenue
Washington D.C.

Dear Mr. President;

As Salaam Alaikum (Peace be unto you).

It is with sincere pride and admiration that we greet you as we continue to monitor your approach to the scourges of terrorism, which have left an indelible mark on the lives of the entire human race.

Mr. President, the events of September 11th have impacted the lives of the American people and members of friendly countries who sought to share the American dream for the betterment of their families and their country.

This impact has been significant, as the entire spectrum of humanity was affected. The disaster was all encompassing of race, creed, colour, religious persuasion and social standing.

As an American Muslim appointed as the International Ambassador representing the Universal Islamic Centre in Jamaica and the wider Caribbean region, the events have been particularly disturbing as the Islam which we embraced for over 25 years and have sought to teach, in no way shape or form condones, supports or associates itself with hatred, terrorism or callous atrocities against innocent human beings. To the contrary Mr. President, the way of life in Islam embraces Peace and Love for humanity.

President Bush, we live for the day when people, irrespective of persuasion, religion, class or colour will unite for Global Oneness and punctuate the motto of "Out of Many One". We live for the day when differences between people and nations will be of no more significance than the colour of the blood, which permeates all our veins.

We are convinced Mr. President that the same ignorance which breeds terrorist activities is the same strain and potency which stimulate and drive hate crimes in every other sect

Attn: President Bush
November 27, 2001
Page 2

of race, colour, religion and class and causes the deep divide in human relations and places responsibility on nations to create and effect "foreign policy" to achieve harmonious relationships.

Sir, unfortunately, in our lifetime Global Oneness may not be achieved, but we can sow the seeds, and we believe that only through education that transcends certification will we really be able to temper or control the "Isms" that inspire human beings to be their worst enemies.

We believe that an "enlightened foreign policy" for our Great Nation should be based on, and targeted toward education that inform and fosters justice, unity and peace for all.

Mr. President, we have chosen to pen these few lines to you because we truly believe that if ever there is a chance for Global Unity and Peace, the time is now and the leader is in place. Your handling of events since September 11th is an inspiration to us all and today we know that with yourself, your team and your Universal allies we can feel confident that the world is in safe hands.

May Almighty ALLAH (GOD) continue to bestow HIS Blessings upon you.

Once again we salute you with the Muslim greeting of Peace As Salaam Alaikum.(Peace be unto you).

Kindest regards,
GLOBAL ONENESS

Douglas Owen-Ali

IMAM DOUGLAS OWEN-ALI
Chairman

United States Department of State

Bureau of Western Hemisphere Affairs
Washington, D.C. 20520-6258

December 21, 2001

Imam Douglas Owen-Ali
Executive Chairman
Global Oneness, Inc.
30 Havendale Drive
Kingston 19
Jamaica WI

Dear Imam Owen-Ali:

I am writing in response to your letter of November 27, 2001 to President George W. Bush. We thank you for your expression of support, on behalf of Global Oneness, for President Bush, and the United States.

As you noted, the events of September 11th have truly been tragic. Yet in the aftermath of such barbaric acts, it is heartwarming to receive such encouraging expressions of friendship and hope for a better world.

Thank you for your kind letter to the President.

Sincerely,

Marsha B. Barnes
Director
Office of Caribbean Affairs
Department of State

'Diplomatic miracle' still possible – *Muslim ambassador*

A SPOKESMAN for the local Muslim community, Ambassador Imam Douglas Owen-Ali, founder and executive chairman of the Global Oneness Organisation and ambassador for the Nation of Islam in Jamaica, says that despite the commencement of war in Iraq a "diplomatic miracle" was still possible.

In a statement yesterday, Imam Owen-Ali, who is also an international ambassador of peace, representing the Universal Islamic Centre of America in Jamaica and the Caribbean, called for special prayers to be offered around the world by people of all religious faiths for peace, healing and reconciliation. Also, he called on the Iraqi regime to offer a genuine spirit of co-operation and comply "to the full unconditional disarmament demands of the United Nations."

His message read:
"As a Muslim and a citizen of the United States of America,

OWEN-ALI

guided and committed to the righteous tenets of Islam, the Divine Injunctions of the Holy Qur'an and the Sunnah (traditions) of the Holy Prophet Muhammad (peace be upon Him), humbly offer the following message.

"I call for all well-thinking Muslims around the world, Christians, Jews and people of all religious faiths to offer special prayers of peace, healing and reconciliation in this on-going conflict between the United States of America and Iraq. The mission of building bridges of understanding, humanity and hope between peoples and nations must now be creatively pursued if human life on all sides is to remain sacrosanct.

"The United States of America has been blessed with a divine trust from Almighty Allah (God) to be the only remaining Global Super Power. Now more than any other time in world history, she has to exemplify humanity and moral leadership to the world community and avoid squandering the outpouring of international goodwill and support it received after the horrific tragedy of September 11, 2001. America now has a glorious opportunity to be a merciful and compassionate super power. Can and will she now grasp this unique moment in history?

"I strongly suggest to the Iraqi regime that it should act with alacrity and offer a genuine spirit of co-operation and comply with the full, unconditional disarmament demands of the United Nations. The human cost of war is catastrophic. I fervently believe that a diplomatic miracle is still possible.

"War on nations change maps. War on poverty maps change. The price of peace is no easy goal, but it is indeed attainable. War must be a last resort!"

No more war, more hate, it is time for us to liberate.

Freedom, justice, liberty, God's way for humanity.

Let Peace, Faith, Love and Justice reign for all,

Let us now answer a righteous call.

As Salaam Alakium. (peace be unto you).

British High
Commission
Kingston

P.O. Box 575
28 Trafalgar Road
Kingston 10
Jamaica

Tel: (876) 510 0732 FTN 8602 3732
Fax: (876) 511 5303
E-mail: Phil.Sinkinson@fco.gov.uk

05 November 2003

Ambassador ImamDouglas Owen-Ali
Global Oneness Limited
30 Havendale Drive
Kingston 19

Dear Douglas

Global Oneness and Building Bridges World tour 2004

I am writing further to your letter of 15 July 2003 and subsequent conversations with Tony Ridout, First Secretary Chancery and myself. I can confirm that we are content in principle to support your Global Oneness and Building Bridges visit to the UK and could assist in the co-ordination of a programme for your visit. Wherever possible we will help to facilitate introductions to Islamic leaders and institutions under the principals outlined in your upcoming publication 'Islam – Building Bridges of Understanding : A Jamaican Voice of Unity'.

You and I agreed that you would make contact with those people we have identified and you would then let me have your comprehensive proposals for onward transmission to those Islamic institutions identified who have expressed interest in meeting with you.

With best wishes

Phil

Phil Sinkinson
Deputy High Commissioner

IN FOCUS | www.jamaica-gleaner.com   THE SUNDAY GLEANER · MAY 2, 2004   G3

Building bridges is the way forward - *Muslim ambassador*

Balford Henry
News Editor

From left to right, Louis Farrakhan, Ainsley Henriques, and Imam Douglas Owen-Ali making peace at the Jewish synagogue last year.

> *What can emerge out of this crisis is a... glorious opportunity once again to build bridges of understanding, humanity and hope*

BUILDING BRIDGES

RELIGIOUS TOLERANCE

WINNING THE PEACE

Muhammad Ali
"The Greatest of All Time"

◄

Imam Ali and the World Champion of peace, Muhammad Ali in Los Angeles, California

Imam Ali and Muhammad Ali at a dinner reception in San Diego, California.

►

◄

Imam Ali with "The Greatest of all time" Muhammad Ali sharing a very special moment.

◄

Imam Ali's sister Cecile with "The Greatest of all time" Muhammad Ali in Los Angeles California.

Ambassador Ali and the Greatest of all time Muhammad Ali join former Jamaica boxing Champion Lloyd Honeyghan in Las ▼ Vagas.

Muhammad Ali celebrating his ▲ 45th birthday on January 17, 1987 at the Hilton Kingston in Jamaica. The reception was hosted by famous boxing promoter Mr. Don King, who received the Martin Luther King Humanitarian Award. (L-R) Muhammad Ali, Imam Ali and Jamaican Business man Mr. Claude Clarke.

►

Muhammad Ali (centre) with manager Jabir Muhammad (left) and road manager Abuwi Mahdi (right).

28th February 1989

The Honorable Michael Manley
Jamaica House
Kingston, Jamaica / British West Indies

Dear Mr. Prime Minister:

Congratulations on your return to the helm of the
Jamaican government.

This letter is written as legal counsel to Muhammad
Ali and it concerns the Children's Peace Mission to
Jamaica being coordinated by your able representative, Mr. Douglas Owen. Mr. Owen has brought to
our attention the serious plight of thousands of
poor Jamaican children desparately in need of
humanitarian assistance.

The Jamaican people are very close to Mr. Ali's
heart, and he has commented frequently regarding
his personal friendship with you and the warm
hospitality extended him on his last visit there.

In the ring, Ali battled men. Today, he fights a
greater battle, one against the common enemies of
mankind----poverty, disease, war and injustice. He
has recently completed a fact-finding tour of the
Sudan and Pakistan, where he visited many severly
depressed areas. And as his attorney, I witnessed
similar hardship in our own hemisphere in Haiti,
dispensing food and supplies to suffering children.

It is our understanding Mr. Owen will coordinate
public relations efforts to bring the Children's
Peace Mission to Jamaica, and that he will work
closely with your government and us to implement
this undertaking in order to bring the focus of
world attention upon the plight of those now
suffering in Jamaica and other regions of the
Caribbean.

In this regard, the undersigned plans to visit
Jamaica on March 15th, with the hope of having Mr.
Ali follow soon thereafter. In the meantime, we
send kind regards to you and your countrymen.

Respectfully yours,

RICHARD HIRSCHFELD
As Counsel To
Muhammad Ali

RH/ms

100 Court Square • Charlottesville, VA 22901 • (804) 977-8000

Imam Ali's Religious Side

Imam Ali at the Islamic Cultural Centre in New York in 2001.

Imam Ali and members of his delegation at the Islamic Cultural Centre of New York in 2001.

▲ *Delivering the Khutbah (sermon) at Jumah Prayer Service at G15 Summit in Montego Bay, Jamaica 1999.*

Delivering the Khutbah (Sermon) at The Juma Service at Muhammad Mosque in Kingston, Jamaica. ►

◄ *Muslims attending Jumah Prayer service at G15 Summit in Montego Bay, Jamaica in 1999.*

FLAIR MAGAZINE Monday, May 28, 2001

Imam Douglas Owen-Ali
Muslim for life

By Barbara Ellington
Flair Co-ordinator

IMAM (SPIRITUAL teacher) Douglas Owen-Ali converted to Islam 25 years ago and as a servant of Allah, does not see himself leaving the religion because although raised in a Christian home "I was never a Christian," said the 44-year-old.

Flair interviewed Mr. Owen-Ali following his recent initiative to encourage investments from the Gulf States into Jamaica. He holds a Bachelors degree in Political Science from City University of New York and a Masters degree in International Law and Public Relations from the University of Lagos in Nigeria.

Of the Nigerian experience, the author/consultant, speaks in glowing terms: "It was a rich intellectual and cultural experience that was both challenging and rewarding — an experience of love, brotherhood, generosity and friendship that will always be close to my heart."

He said there were enormous similarities between Nigerians and Jamaicans and that though we had been separated by colonialism many of the traditions were still intact.

On the question of his religious experience in Nigeria, Owen-Ali said he had gained more insight into Islam and fervently believed that religion should not divide the people of the world but unite them. He was pleased that recently Pope John Paul became the first Roman Catholic Pope to visit a Muslim mosque in Syria.

"I hope his action helps to unify the world to see that this action could inspire other religious leaders to see this as the way forward for all God's children, because the first principle of Islam is the belief in the oneness of God and every Muslim should subscribe to the belief in God," he said.

Owen-Ali maintains that the Muslim philosophy is one of religious tolerance. "We are all God's children; one humanity regardless of race, colour, creed, ethnicity or religious persuasion and we should embrace the spirit of universal oneness.

But what of Islam and terrorism? Owen-Ali said, "As a practising Muslim who adheres to the Sunnah (tradition of Prophet Muhammad), I condemn terrorism but I also condemn injustice, I have respect for the sanctity of human life."

He went on to express dissatisfaction with the breakdown of the moral values in the Jamaican society and said the time has come for the country to have, "...positive leadership and not merely salesmanship. Leaders must realise that they have a divine trust from God/Allah which they should not abandon.

THE MAN/WOMAN RELATIONSHIP IN ISLAM

The Muslim attitude of men to women is based on the teachings of their holy book, the Qur'an which espouses full respect for women.

"The Prophet Muhammad gave full, equal and civic rights to Jews and Christians living in Medina and Saudi Arabia and he also gave the same rights to women so contrary to international public opinion, the divine principles of the Muslim religion accords women full respect," said Owen-Ali.

He noted that in many cultures women are regarded as second class citizens creating a religious cultural paradox but that was not the case in the religion he follows.

ISLAMIC MARRIAGE

On marriage, Owen-Ali said Muslims are allowed to have four wives but this is a cultural not a religious practice. Divorce is not encouraged but is used as a last resort.

The section of the Qur'an that deals with marriage, states in part, "Allah created men and women so that they can provide company to one another, love one another, procreate children and live in peace and tranquillity,

to the commandments of Allah and the directions of his messenger.

Described as a friend of the unbefriended poor by Professor Ibrahim Gambari, Permanent Representative of Nigeria to the United Nations, Owen-Ali is currently at the forefront of Global Oneness. As its founder and executive chairman he said one of the objectives of Global Oneness was to highlight the plight of innocent children.

The organisation sees its mission as helping to put in place facilities to provide shelter, food, education and health services for neglected children in Jamaica and the region.

Owen-Ali's goals include working to develop more meaningful relationships between Jamaica, the African continent and the Middle East and the Muslim world.

"There are tremendous benefits to be gained economically, commercially and culturally," he said. He also hopes to continue to strive to achieve righteousness and to work as a shepherd for the world's less fortunate. "I will not rest until there is justice for every race and equality in every place."

Owen-Ali is married and has one daughter. In his spare time he loves to dance, listen to music, write poetry, watch football and athletics.

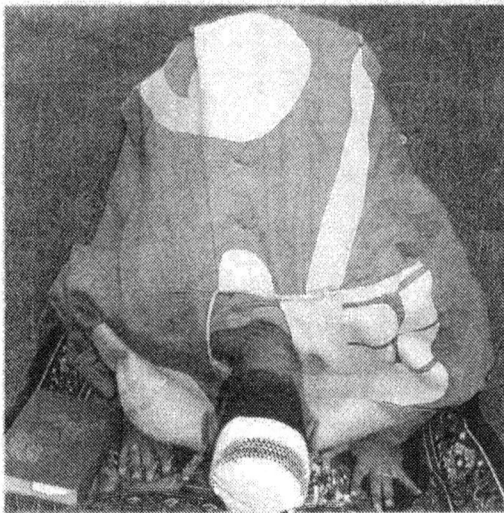

IAN ALLEN/ *Staff Photographer*

Imam Owen-Ali seen here praying. Some Muslims in Jamaica worship on Fridays at either the Majid as-Salaam on Leicester Avenue in Kingston or at the Central Masjid on Camp Road.

Building Bridges with the Motherland: The African Connection

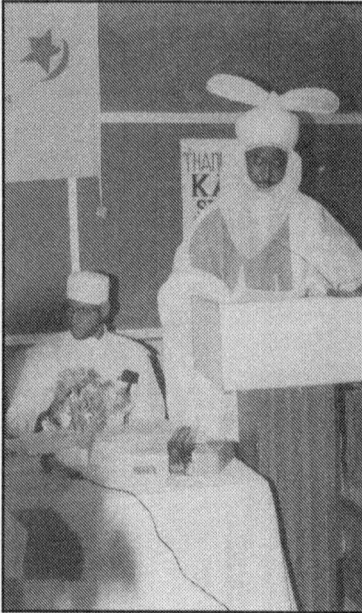

Imam Ali with His Highness Tafidan Kano Alhaji Nasiru Bayero at book launching ceremony in Kano, State Nigeria in 1994.

"The African Connection"
Imam Ali presents a copy of his earlier book to His Highness Alhaji Ado Bayero The Emir of Kano. This presentation took place at the Emir's Palace in Kano State, Nigeria.

"The African Connection"
Imam Ali presenting a gift to Nigerian business tycoon the late Alhaji Chief M.K.O. Abiola at the University of Lagos in Nigeria.

People's Voice

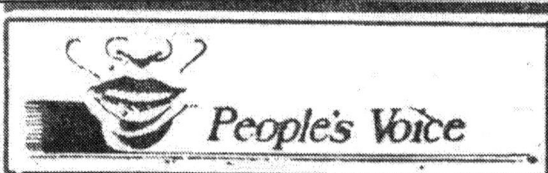

Thank you, Alhaji Folawiyo

WHEN I accepted a commonwealth post graduate scholarship to study in Nigeria, people told me I was crazy. They abounded me with tales. Some of which scared the day lights out of me. Lion-hearted that I am, I said 'seeing is believing'. In July of 1992 I arrived in Lagos, Nigeria.

My dreams soon became my worst nightmares. The scholarship award, oiled by inflation dwindled. Confusion attended my living arrangements and soon I would be on the street with my bags, no place to stay and no airline ticket. The academic programme was also in trouble, the result of strike and counter strikes. For a course of study which should take one year I have so far had two months of lectures.

I was disillusioned and confused. A return to my country without completing the course of study would be greeted with ridicule and cynicism punctuated by 'I told you Nigeria was bad news'. My depleted financial reserve meant that it was either I returned home and spread the bad news or look for a good Samaritan. My search led me up many blind allies, until finally it led me to a place in Lagos called 'Unity House'.

There I found unity, hope, brotherhood, sincerity and philanthropy. Benevolence is an inadequate expression to describe the golden hand shake which I received in the form of a generous endowment compliments of Dr. Wahab Iyanda 'Yinka" Folawiyo O.F.R.

Thanks to this pride of Nigeria. Baba Adinni of Nigeria, I will be able to stay in Nigeria and pursue my intellectual ambition.

Chief Folawiyo's philanthropy, benevolence, and sincerity are surpassed only by his humility. I have discovered that thousands of persons and hundreds of institutions and organizations have been the beneficiary of his calculated generosity. The lesser deeds of many scream from the pages and electronic waves of the media. This gentleman asks for no more than the opportunity to exercise the will of Almighty Allah.

Imam Douglas Owen-Ali, Post Graduate School, Faculty of Law, Unversity of Lagos.

Organisation de la Conférence Islamique
Mission Permanente d'Observateur
aupres des Nations Unies

بسم الله الرحمن الرحيم

Organization of the Islamic Conference
Permanent Observer Mission
to the United Nations

MEMBER STATES OF THE
ORGANIZATION OF THE ISLAMIC CONFERENCE

1.	AFGHANISTAN	28.	MALAYSIA
2.	ALBANIA	29.	MALDIVES
3.	ALGERIA	30.	MALI
4.	AZERBAIJAN	31.	MAURITANIA
5.	BAHRAIN	32.	MOROCCO
6.	BANGLADESH	33.	MOZAMBIQUE
7.	BENIN	34.	NIGER
8.	BRUNEI DARUSSALAM	35.	NIGERIA
9.	BURKINA FASO	36.	OMAN
10.	CAMEROON	37.	PAKISTAN
11.	CHAD	38.	PALESTINE
12.	COMOROS	39.	QATAR
13.	DJIBOUTI	40.	SAUDI ARABIA
14.	EGYPT	41.	SENEGAL
15.	GABON	42.	SIERRA LEONE
16.	GAMBIA	43.	SOMALIA
17.	GUINEA	44.	SUDAN
18.	GUINEA-BISSAU	45.	SURINAME
19.	INDONESIA	46.	SYRIA
20.	IRAN	47.	TAJIKISTAN
21.	IRAQ	48.	TOGO
22	JORDAN	49.	TUNISIA
23.	KAZAKHASTAN	50.	TURKEY
24.	KUWAIT	51.	TURKMENISTAN
25.	KYRGYZSTAN	52.	UGANDA
26.	LEBANON	53.	UNITED ARAB EMIRATES
27.	LIBYA	54.	UZBEKISTAN
		55.	YEMEN

OBSERVER STATES

1. BOSNIA & HERZEGOVINA
2. CENTRAL AFRICAN REPUBLIC
3. GUYANA
4. TURKISH MUSLIM COMMUNITY
    OF CYPRUS

130 East 40th Street, (5th floor), New York, N.Y. 10016
Telephone: (212) 883-0140   Telex: 234524   OCIC UR   Fax: (212) 870-3009

These group of countries make up the Organization of Islamic Conference. The Organization of Islamic Conference (OIC) is an international organization grouping fifty five states which have decided to pool their resources together, combine their efforts and speak with voice to safeguard the interests and secure the progress and well-being of their peoples and all Muslims in the world.

P.OA Sunday Herald

INTERNATIONAL   October 4, 1998

A new hope for Nigeria

By Imam Douglas Owen-Ali

On Thursday, September 24, General Abdulsalami A. Abubakar, the new Head of State, of Nigeria, addressed the fifty-third session of The United Nations General Assembly in New York. It was a moving speech that brought an enthusiastic response by all the member states, in particular the African group.

Events under the past two military administrations make Nigerians cautious, even cynical, but that is understandable. However, the bold, courageous and sincere initiatives now being pursued by General Abubakar towards the achievement of a lasting and viable democracy, peace, justice, economic reforms and human rights, a new hope and a new beginning has emerged in Nigeria.

At a reception to honor General Abubakar at the Waldorf Astoria Hotel in New York, a Nigerian aptly described their new leader, as the "bus stop." General Abubakar remarked at the reception: "It is good to see Nigerians smiling again." Justice, declared General Abubakar,

in his landmark address to Nigeria and the world about his mission, on July 20, of this year, "will not only be done, it will seem to be done." He has positively demonstrated a willingness, not merely to preach, but to act — starting with himself. He has already declared his assets, promising to do so again before vacating office next year.

United States President Bill Clinton met with General Abubakar in Washington recently, to discuss matters of mutual interest. Such an honor has not been accorded a Nigerian leader for 17 years.

General Abubakar concluded his address to the United Nations General Assembly with the following remarks: "A silent but peaceful revolution is taking place in Nigeria. Our people are determined to ensure that sustainable democratic governance is established in the country. Nigeria is clearly at the threshold of a new beginning in its domestic political and socio-economic structure, and foreign relations agenda. This is the time, therefore, for the international community to give the necessary encouragement and support for our endeavours."

OPINION   THE DAILY OBSERVER Saturday, May 25, 1996 Page 7

Jamaica-Nigeria relations: I think we're wrong on this one

IT is with much regret that Jamaica-Nigeria relations is now at an all-time low. The government of Jamaica recently declared sanctions against the federal military government of Nigeria, headed by General Sani Abacha.

I write as a concerned citizen of Jamaica and as a true friend of Nigeria. I must first take this opportunity to extend my profound appreciation and gratitude to the many people in Nigeria for their kind generosity, love and goodwill expressed to me during my stay there, where I successfully completed post-graduate studies in International Law and Diplomacy at the University of Lagos. Special thanks must also go to my benefactor in Nigeria, Chief Folawiyo, The Baba Adinni of Nigeria for keeping my dream alive. I have indeed come home from the bosom of my African family.

Jamaica and Nigeria have both enjoyed cordial and positive diplomatic relations for over 20 years, based on the diplomatic principles of mutual respect, tolerance and reciprocity.

During this period, Nigeria had several military regimes. Formal diplomatic ties between both countries began under the military regime of former head of state, General Yakubu Gowon. Except for the period 1979-1983 under former civilian president, Alhaji Shehu Shagari, Nigeria has had successive military regimes. It would be, therefore, appropriate to conclude that current military rule is not unique to Nigeria, but rather an integral part of that country's political culture.

The sanctions imposed by the government of Jamaica are in the following areas:

• visa requirements for Nigerians coming to Jamaica;

• the Bilateral Technical Aid Co-operation Programme (TAC);

• a ban on sporting contracts with official Nigerian delegations and teams;

• no military contact with Nigeria;

• the non-appointment of a Jamaican high commissioner to Nigeria at this time.

The imposition of these sanctions by the government of Jamaica may not go down well with the Abacha military regime. While such measures may have been devised with good intentions in mind, this will not hasten the democratic timetable of the military. What it may accomplish is an extreme response. Another area of critical diplomatic concern is the non-appointment of a Jamaican high commissioner to Nigeria at this time. An ambassador on the ground would be in a better position to have constructive diplomatic dialogue through quiet, but persuasive diplomacy. Without such representation, the diplomatic initiative is lost. Successful diplomatic relations between countries are achieved through reciprocity, not animosity.

It would therefore, best serve Jamaica's foreign policy interests on the continent of Africa and their wider national-economic interests to review its foreign-policy position vis-a-vis Nigeria. While the present measures will not have any negative economic or political impact on either country, as commercial and trade relations are at present negligible, it is bound to impact negatively on

the people of both countries in respect of future cultural and educational exchanges.

The Jamaican government should also take into account that Nigeria has been a friend over the years and have offered us much needed moral and material support. They must also remember Nigeria's prominent role in liberation struggles throughout Africa, including the anti-apartheid movement. While they may disagree with the present military regime, it would be advisable to look at the prospect from an enlightened perspective, in order to communicate and to arrive at an accurate foreign policy position. I must also add, that unless our foreign policy decision-makers strive to understand the political and cultural complexities of African politics, diplomatic blunders will occur, regardless of the African countries involved.

While no one can condone human rights abuses in Nigeria, or the execution of Ken Saro-Wiwa and eight others last year, there must still be a sincere attempt to pursue the diplomatic initiative through mutual respect, mutual tolerance and constructive dialogue. Jamaica should prepare itself to deal with a post-Abacha regime, and if diplomatic relations are destroyed between both countries, it will be very difficult to repair such relations within a reasonable time. I may also note that Nigeria has already responded to the measures taken by Jamaica in respect of the Technical Aid Co-operation Programme and the visa requirements for Jamaicans planning to visit

Nigeria.

There are two areas that will no doubt impact negatively, not only on the diplomatic relations of both countries, but even more importantly, on the cultural and social relationship between our people. The time has now come for Jamaica to develop a meaningful and constructive African Policy, not in words, but in deeds.

It is not sufficient to boast of being a predominantly black country when the occasion permits, but rather we should all strive sincerely towards the goal of Universal African and Black Unity. Nigeria, regardless of its problems and complexities, is still the giant of the African continent. We hear stories about corruption and dishonesty in and outside of Nigeria, but the truth of the matter is that the majority of Nigerians are hard-working, decent people. Jamaica and Nigeria, as a matter of urgency, should work towards a healing. We are one family, we may have to disagree to ultimately agree. The government of Jamaica should offer Nigeria a helping hand so that country moves towards a lasting democracy.

If Jamaica is to remain sincere to the future liberation of all Africa, and to African struggles and causes around the globe and the indelible legacy of our own illustrious son, Marcus Mosiah Garvey and his prophetic vision of ONE GOD, ONE AIM, ONE DESTINY, Nigeria should not be ignored nor isolated. Let us offer our hand of brotherhood, friendship, patience and understanding. The right signals should also be communicated, so as to not only normalise diplomatic relations, but to improve them.

By Douglas Owen-Ali

ONLY IN NIGERIA

By Imam Douglas Owen-Ali

BAD news travels fast, far and wide, spreading distrust, suspicion and avoidance. Good news get sidelined and down played. This is true in the case of Nigeria. The international perception is that greed, trickery and chicanery is as vast as the population, colourful as the clothing and loves it way like that agbada.

When I accepted a commonwealth post graduate scholarship to study in Nigeria, people looking at me crazy. They abounded me with tales, some of which scared the day lights out of me. I am hearted that I am, I said "seeing is believing." On July of 1982 I arrived in Lagos, Nigeria.

My dreams soon became my worst nightmares. The scholarship award, oiled by inflation deindexed Confusion attended my living arrangements and soon I would be on the street with my bags, no place to stay and no status.

fickel. The academic programme was also in trouble. The result of strike and counter strikes. For a course study which should take one year I have so far had two months of lectures.

I was disillusioned and confused. A return to my country without completing the course of study would be greeted with ridicule and cynicism punctuated by "I TOLD YOU NIGERIA WAS BAD NEWS." My depleted financial reserve meant that it was either I returned home and spread the bad news or look for a good Samaritan. My search lead me to many black allies, until finally it led to a place in Lagos called "UNITY HOUSE."

There I found unity, hope, brotherhood, sincerity and philanthropy. Benevolence is an inadequate expression to describe the golden hand shake which I received in the form of generous endowment and gifts of Alhaji Chief

Dr. Waheb Iyanda "Vinka" Folawiyo O.F.R. Thanks to the pride of Nigeria, Baba Adinni of Nigeria, I will be able to stay in Nigeria and pursue my intellectual ambition.

This act of kindness will cement and forge a bond of mutual co-operation and friendship between two black nations (Nigeria and Jamaica) regardless the poverty thousands and kilometres of space. Two Kingdom of Islam will increase as I take the message of hope to the Caribbean. The potential exists that this Baba Adinni of Nigeria, can be crowned Baba Adinni of Jamaica.

Chief Folawiyo's philanthropy, benevolence, and sincerity are surpassed only by

his humility. I have discovered that thousands of peo-

Chief Folawiyo

ators and hundreds of institutions and organizations have been the beneficiary of his calculated generosity.

The lesser deeds of many scream from the pages and electronic waves of the media. This gentleman seeks for no more than the opportunity to transfuse the will of Almighty Allah. He lives the creed "The fortunate is the one who spends and gives away. The unfortunate is the one who dies and leaves behind."

I can think of a very few place in this world which produce men who embrace and express the tenets of freedom in the way Alhaji Chief Dr. Waheb Iyanda "Vinka" Folawiyo does. Nigeria, indeed Africa, is fortunate to have a such a son.

my good fortune to have stumbled in the path of this great man. I, a stranger from yonder, seasoned in a harsh land, could have perished like man of my kind, but who were bundled into slave ships and carpeted out of this very country across the Atlantic to the Americas and the Caribbean. Sometimes I mumbled "BACK HOME TO OSÉ." Now I say thanks be to Allah God is there. Only in Nigeria have I seen philanthropy, brotherhood and sensitivity of this kind. I must spread the word "THE BABA ADINNI IS INDEED THE FATHER."

Owen-Ali is a Jamaican Commonwealth scholar, pursuing Post Graduate Studies in International Law and Diplomacy at the University of Lagos

My African Dream

My African dream, My African Dream
What will it be?
What is it? My African Dream.

Africa! The Cradle of civilisation
God's crown of creation,
Land of the Black hope, Dream of the Nations,
Oh! You mighty nation
Rich is your story.

Now you are burning hot, people have not
Suffering hopelessness, despair, now seems your lot
Dreams and hopes die and rot
The air pungent, the land barren with dried blood
This is a great shame... Who is to blame?

Mighty Africa rise up!
Nigeria, Ghana, Liberia, Kenya Somalia, Ethiopia
Jamaica, Trinidad, America, North East, West and South
Dream not, slumber not, despair not
March, reclaim your fame, let the drums roll

The Truth must be told, Rise up again
With dignity take your place
The twenty-first century is here.

Mother Africa, be bold, save your soul,
Save your children, be the mighty race
Not the forgotten case
Freedom from economic depression
Justice for every race, equality in every place
One God, One Aim, One Destiny.

My African Dream shall be your reality
Your ultimate reality
My Dream: Your unity
My Dream: Your peace
My Dream: Your progress
My Dream: Your prosperity.

My African Dream, my vision
Your commission to repossess
Your supremacy, your reality,
Your identity, your humanity
Let no one plunder the Black, pearl of nations
Rise! Oh! Africa! Take your place
Rewrite your History,
Rich is your story.

Imam Douglas Owen-Ali,
July 1993

SEPTEMBER 11ᵗʰ
IRONY OR PROPHESY

In August 2001, in Chicago Illinois I had both the honour and distinction of addressing an August gathering of Muslims from around the world, at a symposium to celebrate the life of the Holy Prophet Muhammad (may peace be upon Him). I used this platform to call for a Muslim Unity not only in Jamaica and the Caribbean, but around the world. My presentation rocked the boat as it challenged the wealthy Muslim States to do more, not only for the cause of Islam, but even more important, to allocate their resources for the cause of suffering humanity. Why is there so much poverty in the Muslim and Arab world, when the wealth of oil can provide the resources and conditions for a better standard of living amongst its citizens? I articulated this position with passion and compassion, to many members of my Muslim family it was a fiery speech coming from a fiery Jamaican and Caribbean Islamic Leader. However, my discourse transcended into the International Arena as I used this auspicious platform to call for greater unity and world peace amongst Muslims as well as Non- Muslims. It is either ironic or prophetic, or both as spoke about the conflict and potential conflicts around the world and the perpetuation of very hostile acts of war and complicated conflicts which continue to claim the lives of innocent children, men and women. In essence, I spoke of the tragedies that plagued our human family, "War and Rumors of Wars." Little did I know that some weeks later the tragic and despicable act of September 11th would have manifested in such a horrific manner.

The Speech — 'Call 9/11'

I begin with a quotation from The Secretary General of The United Nations, His Excellency Kofi Annan, in an address to the summit of the Organization of Islamic Conference, in Tehran, Iran on the December 9th, 1997: "Allow me to pay tribute to the Great Faith of Islam. It has ennobled and enriched humanity, throughout its history. Today, it inspires the belief of more than a billion men and women around the world and is a universal spiritual force for humankind. This fact makes it all the more distressing to witness the increasing resort to violence and terror by extremist groups in the name of Islam. They are sullying the image of a religion whose very name signifies peace and whose Almighty Creator is the Compassionate, the Merciful."

The Mission

In a real sense, every individual carries the mandate in their own personal exercise of good citizenry. Every man and woman is an ambassador of their own culture, religion and commerce. I am indeed both honored and humbled to represent the Universal Islamic Center of America and the Nation of Islam in Jamaica and the Caribbean region. I welcome the opportunity and the challenge and I pray for divine guidance from Almighty Allah (God). In the final analysis, the mission is to uplift and enrich the lives of the citizens of the Caribbean spiritually, morally, educationally, economically and culturally. This includes, bringing to Caribbean citizens, an economic and spiritual empowerment that will enlarge their respect for Islam, broaden their exposure to the culture of the Muslim way, and cultivate Taqwah (fear of Allah) even among those not born to Islam.

As an international ambassador of peace, the mission is one of building bridges of humanity and hope for the human family and espousing the ideals of freedom, peace, liberty, justice, enlightened tolerance, dialogue, mutual trust, and mutual acceptance amongst persons of different religious, political, economic and social persuasions. We have successfully started this mission in Jamaica and the Caribbean. A new beginning can and will emerge as we work fervently on building bridges of understanding, humanity and hope for the human family around the world. It is only appropriate that I give a conclusive view of September 11th, Islam, and terrorism, primarily for the purpose of education and information. For this is not my view, as I am only a baby in Islam, but I can confidently say a very strong baby in the faith. I am only a mere student of Islam. The Grand Mufti of the Kingdom of Saudi Arabia, Sheikh Abdul Aziz Abdullah Al-Sheikh reiterated on the day of Arafah and Pilgrimage that "Islam is against terrorism, and urged the Ummah to unite in defense of faith". "It is unfair to associate Islam with terrorism." In a sermon from Al-Namirah Mosque in Arafah, the Grand Mufti said, "terrorism equals tyranny and injustice, and these are alien to Islam." How can terrorism be linked to a religion which orders respect for human life... (a religion which advocates) justice and promotes peace rather than war?' It is utterly "unfair to attribute terrorism to Islam", he said. "Islam strictly forbids killing of women, children and innocent people... it calls for respect of treaties and agreements... and upholds rights at all times," he added.

The Grand Mufti called on the international media to inform the people of the positive aspects of Islam and to serve the causes of the Islamic nations. He also called for an educational curricula that link Muslims with Islam and strengthen their bonds with Almighty Allah. I am confident that this is not just a view, but a Divine interpretation of Islam and the *Holy Qur'an* coming from one of the foremost Islamic scholars in the world. I personally submit myself to the righteousness and Divinity of knowledge which comes from this great Muslim scholar. This is the Islam that I embrace along with all well thinking moderate Muslims around the world. We must stand and let our voices be heard. World Islamic leadership like that of the Grand Mufti of the Kingdom of Saudi Arabia must now echo with the infectious truth of Al-Islam. The extremist voices must be challenged with balance and moderation. They must be challenged with the true Islamic spirit of peace, love, tolerance and universal brotherhood. Salaam Alaikium. (Peace be unto to You). Al Sheikh urged the worlds 1.3 billion Muslims to adhere to their religion. "The Islamic Nations are experiencing momentous events these days, and this requires it to think rationally and unite in defense of its faith", he said. He is the Chairman of the Higher Ulema Council and department of Scientific Research and Ifta he spoke to nearly two million Muslims gathered in Arafah for the climax of Hajj.

Empowerment of Children

The Global Oneness organization, of which I am founder, is committed to the spiritual and economic empowerment of disenfranchised children not only in Jamaica and the wider Caribbean region, but throughout the entire world. Sustainable economic development, educational and humanitarian programmes are of the utmost priority to the Global Oneness Team. We assert that children, around the world, deserve to enjoy the precious gem of freedom. The challenges are real and deep, but I say without reservation every child has an equal right to live and be free, they must not be trapped in the evil shackles of misery and poverty. I remain both passionate and compassionate when it comes to the issue of children.

World leadership in the Christian world, the Jewish world and the Muslim World, and all humanity must now take an active and positive stand by embracing and empowering children with life! The social and economic well being of the world's children needs to be of universal priority. More needs to be done to combat world injustice to suffering and innocent children. This is our mandate at Global Oneness. We will wage war against poverty and injustice to our innocent children. This is an urgent humanitarian necessity. We will also wage war against diseases in regions of the world where the life of a disadvantaged child really has no value. When I see street children in Jamaica having to wipe a car windscreen to purchase basic survival food, this moves me to tears. This is not religion, this is not politics, this is not sensationalism of the media. Let us keep it real, this put plainly is about human indignity and suffering, and one of epic proportions. To my Muslim family around the globe we must constantly be reminded that our beloved Holy Prophet Muhammad (peace be upon Him) was an orphan child. He always showed great compassion and mercy to children particularly those who were orphans. It is pertinent that I share the thoughts of a young Jamaican female student, Stevanie D. D. Mills. A student who attends Wolmer's Prepartory School in Kingston, Jamaica. Her expressions are advocated in a simple and sincere manner. Her brief essay has been a guide to me. It's sincere simplicity, I believe, can also be a guide to our world leaders as they pursue the arduous search for a genuine and lasting world peace.

WHY THE WORLD NEEDS PEACE AND LOVE

"In today's world, PEACE is interpreted wrongly, or is being looked at by many people with different meanings.

My Oxford Dictionary defines peace as doing good to others.

We need to have peace in our hearts, and in our homes, before we can show peace to our brothers and sisters.

Heads of all different nations in the world need to stop fighting against each other and try to help one another.

Our world today is divided due to poverty, racism, war and illiteracy, because we think evil, we speak evil and make our world corrupted with evil.

Please all nations try to give peace a chance, change our societies, countries and nations.

Let peace and love rule in the world.

It is therefore, only appropriate that I close this issue with Introduction c.19 - from the Holy Qur'an which is most relevant and should serve as a guiding light to Muslims and to humanity."

"To the Praiseworthy indeed be praise:
Born in the Sacred City he destroyed
Its superstition; loyal to his people to the core,
He stood for all humanity; orphan-born
And poor, he envied not the rich,
And made his special care all those
Whom the world neglected or oppressed
Orphans, women, slaves, and those in need
Of food or comforts, mental solace, spiritual strength,
Or virtues downtrodden in the haunts of men."

ISLAM AND TERRORISM

As a practicing and devout Muslim guided by The *Holy Qur'an* and The Sunnah (traditions) of The Holy Prophet Muhammad (may peace be upon Him), I must first of all seek to clarify the Islamic position in respect of terrorism. On the morning of September 11th 2001, I was getting prepared to leave from Kingston, Jamaica to Chicago Illinois. I was alerted of the attack on the World Trade Center and of that of the Pentagon while at home. As I turned on the television, I witnessed the planes going into the buildings, I was moved to tears and a immediate chill all over my body. Initially, it was that of a nightmare, there was a feeling of denial. Could this have been a horror movie? My trip, of course, was cancelled, then the news came hours after, that this was a terrorist attack on the United States of America. First of all, I must state with the utmost pride that I am an American Citizen. I cherish both my Jamaican and American experience, I fly both flags with pride. Both countries have had a bond of friendship throughout the years. The great country of America has afforded me the opportunity of a higher education, intellectual enhancement, exposure and upward mobility, and the choice of freedom. America has nurtured my development as a human being. I do not hesitate to say with pride and dignity, "I am an American". I have always stated that I am a product of Jamaica and the Caribbean, but the product was honed and nurtured by the United States of America.

To my mind, I was the first Islamic leader in Jamaica and the Caribbean to issue a public statement unequivocally condemning the attack on the United States of America. This tragedy however, has had its positive impact, it has forged new friendships, it has created a new spirit of dialogue amongst groups that were otherwise apart. I have developed a strong friendship with The Embassy Family of the United States of America in Jamaica, I have also cultivated personal friendships with the Deputy Chief of Mission Mr. Richard Smyth and The Consul General Mr. Donald Wells. Thus, I have had the opportunity of paying an official visit and courtesy call on the United States Ambassador Her Excellency Sue Cobb. I have expressed my friendship and support in a letter to President George W. Bush in the War Against Terrorism. The Islamic Community of Jamaica now has regular dialogue with The Embassy of The United States.

I embrace a religion and a way of life that is dedicated to the principles of peace, compassion, enlightened tolerance, equal rights for all, justice and freedom. The killing of innocent people in the name of Allah (God) is not Islam. I repeat, the killing of innocent people in the name of Allah (God) is not Islam. This evil practice contradicts Islamic Injunctions. It is not the way of our beloved Prophet Muhammad (peace be upon Him). The *Holy Qur'an* does not in any way advocate the killing of innocent people under any circumstances.

Let us not be fooled by some insane misguided extremist calling for Jihad. They should call for a Jihad for their own self purification from their evil deeds. The moderate voices in Islam including myself, must now speak without fear or favor. Prophet Muhammad (peace be upon Him) always spoke of the protection of the innocent lives in times of warfare. The lives of the innocent, the women, the children, the orphans, the elderly must be protected and secured. This is the way of our Prophet. He did not teach hate for anyone and even had dialogue with his arch enemies with a view to securing a peaceful co-existence. Killing innocent people in the name of God is no virtue and will not reward any Muslim a place in Jannah (paradise). I wish to make it very clear in the most unequivocal terms that Islam has no relationship with terrorism. A religion which raised the banner of emancipation of humanity from ignorance and exploitation cannot by any stretch of imagination, promote the bloodshed of innocent victims.

Islam is universal religion; it proclaims unity and peace among the whole human family. It is a religion and way of life of peace and blessings. It has, therefore, nothing to do with terrorism or ill-will. A victorious Islam in Mecca did not seek revenge against its enemies who had imposed violence and tyranny over its adherents. Even in the euphoria of victory, it offered amnesty and peace to all its enemies and opponents. This historical example is evidence enough to prove that Islam is the champion of peace and justice, not of destruction and violence.

Terrorism is not a recent phenomenon. It has existed ever since man has existed. Many regions and nations around the world have suffered from the violence and destruction imposed by terrorism. There is no denying the fact that Terrorism is the enemy of civilized life, of peace, of justice, of liberty, human rights and freedom. The international media projects Islam as a religion of blood thirsty zealots. This is sometimes done out of misguided misinformation, not necessarily in all cases, but, out of a bias against Islam. One who sacrifices his or her life for a just moral cause, or righteous principles is a martyr not a terrorist.

The Reverend Dr. Martin Luther King Jr., recipient of the Nobel Peace Prize, sacrificed his life for a just moral cause. The civil rights movement was based on a righteous principle. Dr. King advocated non-violence and peaceful coexistence amongst human kind. Former President of South Africa, Dr. Nelson Mandela sacrificed twenty eight years of his life in prison for a just moral cause, the fight against Apartheid. Yet, even in his divine victory, he called for the principles of reconciliation and healing for the nation South Africa. Neither Dr. King nor Dr. Mandela resorted to hatred, divisiveness or retaliation.

I was asked to deliver a lecture in celebration of African American History Month in February 2002, at the Embassy of the United States, in Kingston, Jamaica. My central theme was "Justice with Dignity". I implored young high school students to stand up for justice, but to do so with dignity, not with hatred and animosity. I implored them to stand up and be counted as valuable and productive human beings, but to do this with class and decorum. I remember listening to a speech by the famous actor and civil rights activist Dr. Harry Bellafonte (O.J.) who articulated to an August gathering at the University of the West Indies "that poverty is no excuse, for the absence of class".

To the extremist forces in Islam who promote terror and the killing of innocent human beings, I must remind them this is not the way of Islam. It is certainly not the way of the Prophet (peace be upon Him). It is not the divine message of The *Holy Qur'an*. Those who embrace the evil spirit of terror, destruction and violence and the killing of innocent people have deviated from the pristine purity of the faith. Please remember sin is sin, a difference of person, of place, does not in any way mitigate the weight of the sin. Terrorism remains terrorism, irrespective of place, section and the society of its origin. It is patently unfair to wrap a terrorist in religious attire. A terrorist is a terrorist, be he an Islamic terrorist, a Christian terrorist, a Hindu terror-ist, a Chinese terrorist, an American terrorist or a Jamaican terrorist. In simple terms, terrorism cannot be confined to any single religious group. The act of violence has no religious tag. It is a human nature or characteristic. War is not necessarily initiated by religion, but rather by dislike. Dislike, in most cases, is born out of injustice. This dislike then turns to hatred.

So, as we address the issue of terrorism and prepare to fight the war against terror and terrorism, it is appropriate to exam-ine the root causes and symptoms of this evil monster, called terror. I have written to the President of the United States of America George W. Bush expressing my full support for the global fight against terrorism. I have called for an "enlightened foreign policy" for our great nation of America, targeted toward education that fosters justice, peace and unity for all. I have called for a world where universal justice must now be the goal; if the human family is to have more harmonious relationships. The great country of the United States now has a glorious opportunity to inspire the true spirit of enduring freedom for the entire planet. It is also a challenge for that great nation to rise above their own permanent national interest and advocate policies for the interest of humanity. America can now become the beacon of light, hope and freedom for the world.

As we correct world injustice and poverty, we will defeat the climate for terror and terrorism to survive. Terrorists and terrorism do not survive in stable countries where people enjoy a good standard of living. They survive in an environment where frustrations are great and people see no way out.

President George W. Bush in the State of the Union address of 2002, advocated an initiative to inspire Islamic economic development in Islamic countries plagued with poverty. This is a vivid example of "enlightened foreign policy". September 11th has indeed not only changed America, but it has also changed the entire world. This unfortunate tragedy brought the great nation of America together as one. "E Pluribus Unus" the motto being "Out of Many, One". Can America remain one United Nation? This is the long term challenge. Will ethnic and racial divisions be something of the past? This is a great challenge. Can America deliver the dream, to all of its of citizens, of life, liberty and the pursuit of happiness, irrespective of race, religion or ethnic origin? Can democracy and freedom become the model for not only the free world, but areas of the world which have been dominated by oppressive dictatorial regimes. The challenges are real, the challenges are deep, but we must fight the scourge of poverty, disease, debt, hopelessness and injustice.

I am reminded of the great and profound words of the late Reverend Dr. Martin Luther King Jr. a champion of peace and justice who so eloquently articulated "injustice anywhere is a threat to justice everywhere". Prophet Muhammad (peace be upon Him) aptly warned "beware of injustice, for injustice will be equivalent to darkness on the day of judgement". Any lasting world peace can only be achieved through dialogue and justice. "Justice for every race, equality in every place, freedom from economic depression" must now become the guiding policy of all nations, rich and poor alike. This call must echo right across planet earth.

I am now moved to quote from the Holy Qur'an Surah 2 Al Baqarah C. 52 (2:254-283) an explanation in respect of charity and good works,

> *"Who can describe the nature of Allah?*
> *The Living, the Eternal: His Throne*
> *Extends over worlds and worlds*
> *That no imagination can compass.*
> *His truth is clear as daylight: how*
> *Can compulsion advance religion?*
> *The keys of Life and Death, and the mysteries*
> *Of everything around us, are in His hands.*
>
> *Our duty then is to seek the path*
> *Of goodness, kindness, upright*
> *Conduct and Charity-to grasp.*
> *At no advantage from a brother's need,*
> *To stand by the word that is pledged,*
> *To bear witness, and remove all cause*
> *Of misunderstandings in our dealings*
> *As between man and man."*

This is the pristine purity of the Islamic way of life as pre-scribed in the Holy Qur'an and the Sunnah (traditions) of the Holy Prophet Muhammad (peace be upon Him). Can the Muslim world live in word and deed, this model of humanity? I challenge my Islamic family around the globe to live this righteous principle. This is also the way of Christianity and Judaism and people of all religious faiths. We must strive to enjoin what is right and forbid what is wrong. Islam places both mercy and forgiveness side by side with justice. As a student of Islam and as an Islamic leader, I am once again moved to emphatically refer to the Holy Qur'an which serves as the righteous guide to all well thinking Muslims. I quote Surah 3 Al 'Imran Ayhat (verse 110),

74

"Ye are the best
Of Peoples, evolved
For mankind,
Enjoining what is right,
Forbidding what is wrong,
And believing in Allah.434
If only the People of the Book
Had faith, it were best
For them: among them
Are some who have faith,
But most of them
Are perverted transgressors."

Islam thus commands (1) faith, (2) doing right, and being an example to others to do right, and having the power to see that right prevails. Having the power to see that wrong and injustice are defeated. The logical conclusion to the evolution of religious history is a non-sectarian, non-racial, non-doctrinal, universal religion, which Islam claims to be. Islam is just submission to the will of Allah (God). I say to the perpetuators of international terrorism who claim to be Muslims, you have deviated from the purity of the Islamic faith, you have become what the *Holy Qur'an* calls "perverted transgressors." One of the major sins in Islam is the killing of innocent people. The *Qur'an* says, "if a man kills an innocent person, to God it looks like he is killing all the innocent people on earth, if you save an innocent person, it looks to God that you are saving all life on earth". The opinion rests on the *Qur'an* chapter 60 verse 8 which bids Islamic victors to "show (civilians) kindness and deal with them justly. "In the Hadiths, or traditions of the prophet Muhammad (peace be upon Him) the prophet commands, "Neither kill the old... nor children, and babes nor the females," This is the Islam that we embrace, a way of life that commands us with mercy and compassion for innocent people even in time of conflict.

Islam is pluralistic in nature as the *Qur'an* says that God created humans different from one another, not to despise each other, but rather to learn from the diversity of one another. To those extremists, our prophet even had dialogue with the infidels. He did not engender hate or disrespect for them. He employed the art of gentle persuasion and diplomacy.

September 11th was an attack not only on the United States of America, but it was an attack on all civilized humanity. It was an attack against all freedom loving people around the world. May I also indicate, hundreds of innocent Muslims were also killed.

I say once again, evil has no religious tag, evil is real, and the evil doers will always disguise themselves usually in the name of religion.

Islam is now the fastest growing religious faith in America and the world. There are approximately eight million Muslims in America from diverse ethnic groups. There are 1.25 billion Muslims around the globe. Many of us, like myself, can be regarded as sane moderate Muslims who take the middle path, but like in any other religious faith or group, there are the insane extremists who seek to engender hate and destruction for humanity. We must fight this evil monster whenever and wherever it appears. President George W. Bush has made it emphatically clear, from the onset that this is not a "War on Islam" it is a war against terrorism. We must support a just international campaign against terrorism, if universal freedom is to be achieved. Terrorist cells can appear even in small countries like Jamaica where poverty is prevalent and will bring destruction to innocent people. No country can now isolate itself from the potential dangers of international terrorism. It is real! It is evil!

President George W. Bush in his State of the Union Address of 2002 spoke passionately of Islam's rich history of Peace and Tolerance, respect for women and the positive contribution of Islam to world civilization. These views articulated by a United States President and a leader of the free world, cannot and must not be viewed as a war against Islam. It shows a view of maturity and respect for the Islamic faith. The President also advocated support, for development and economic opportunity in the Islamic world. This policy is critical in the fight against terrorism for, as long as people are trapped by the scourge of poverty, hopelessness and injustice, the terrorist will no doubt manipulate these conditions. As we fight to preserve and cultivate freedom around the world, we must use the resources of the developed world to bring economic dignity to the marginalized majority of the world. We must also use the weapon of economic upliftment to bring about not only a safer and more secure world, but a world where the disparities between the "haves" the "have nots" and those who may never have, are reduced significantly. As we strive to preserve the sanctity of human life in the United States of America and around the world, we must also strive to preserve the right of every member of the human family to a decent standard of economic life. Our global vision must be a mission of possibilities which will result in freedom, justice and equality for all. In short, physical freedom and economic freedom must now go hand in hand, if world democracy is to be enhanced and the extremist views of international terror and terrorism are to be isolated and subsequently defeated. Let us turn the table, for I know we are able. God has given us the will power to change every hour. Man has advanced to outer space, now we must advance the cause of the human race. Man has achieved technological supremacy, but we are yet to acknowledge our common humanity. Globalization must practically benefit both the developed world and the developing world. "Prosperity must be the goal for every human soul." Every man, woman and child must have an equal right to live.

September 11th has no doubt transformed the world, but we must use this horrific tragedy to create a climate of positive ideals that will foster democracy, world peace, universal justice, freedom, liberty and the economic rebirth for human kind.

The leadership of the United States of America and the free world now has a glorious opportunity to promote foreign policies that are enlightened and just. With this enlightened leadership, coupled with military, economic and diplomatic options, humankind will be given the opportunity to together march to the mountain top of freedom, peace, justice and prosperity.

THE GLOBAL ONENESS MISSION. BUILDING BRIDGES OF UNDERSTANDING, HUMANITY AND HOPE.

THE PRICE OF PEACE. (July 4th 2002)

I begin this segment by acknowledging the bold and sincere efforts of Her Excellency, Sue Cobb The United States Ambassador to Jamaica, and the Deputy Chief of Mission, Mr. Richard Smyth, along with the able and committed staff at the Embassy in the pursuit of building bridges of understanding humanity and hope in Jamaica. As I write, it is now July 4th, 2002 celebrating 226 years of America's independence. We pray fervently that this celebration will be free of any form of hostility around the world. In Jamaica, we will once again celebrate the bond of friendship and good will between both countries. I take this opportunity to personally commend, Ambassador Sue Cobb and her husband former Ambassador Charles E. Cobb Jr. and the entire United States Embassy Family in Jamaica for hosting a splendid July 4th celebration which could be aptly described "as a memorable evening with distinguished people." May the spirit, light of freedom and liberty transcend beyond the shores of the United States of America and may the magnificent words of the Constitution of the Declaration of Independence which guarantees to all men and women the unalienable rights of life, liberty and the pursuit of happiness become a promise not only to the citizens of the United States, but to all members of the human family.

This great promise must be nurtured and made real. Improved communication reduces hostility. Jamaica has always been a close friend and ally of the United States, both countries have enjoyed a bond of mutual friendship and unity for several years. More needs to be done, however, to nurture and enhance the relations between both countries. Again, communication remains a vital tool in achieving this end. Education is also a critical component in the process of building bridges of humanity and hope.

President George W. Bush recently stated that "we Americans must make a stronger case for our humanity around the world." As an American citizen, I humbly recommend that we must do more to highlight the humanity of America. This does not mean that there should be some high powered public relations campaign to promote America's humanity, but rather a public education international campaign to espouse the positive American values such as democracy, freedom of speech, civil liberties and equality of opportunity under the law.

The United States of America can and will enjoy more global friendships, if this great country is perceived as "a caring considerate, and compassionate super power." America now has an enormous responsibility to the future well-being of human kind. The mission of building bridges of understanding, humanity and hope is a universal mission to which I have committed my life work. This is not an Islamic mission, nor a crusade to attract converts to Islam, it is a mission of service to God and to humanity.

The assertion that Islam is the religion of tolerance par excellence often seems preposterous to Western observers. Yet, it is true. The *Qur'an* repeatedly maintains that difference between men and women in terms of colour, wealth, race, language or ethnic origins are natural (30:22); Allah even describes ideological and religious pluralism as God-given: "...and if God had so willed, surely, He could have made you one single community, but (He willed otherwise) in order to test you by what He gave you. Therefore, compete with one another in all virtues." (5:48) The prophet of Islam even predicted that His own community would split into many groups, indulging in excessive pluralism. It is not my intention to engage in theology, but rather to educate Muslims and non-Muslims alike as to the pristine purity of the Islamic faith. It is not good enough to say we believe in Allah (God), but this belief must be supported by knowledge and sincere deeds. Christians, Muslims, Jews and people of all religious faiths have a divine obligation to fulfill the moral law of God. The *Qur'an* says "that Allah (God) has conferred dignity on mankind." From the tragedy of September 11th, there is now an opportunity for humanity to get closer together.

All religious people have one thing in common – to uphold the moral will of Justice. A new moral will must be realized for the salvation of humanity. The essence of Islam, is for the soul of man and woman to be at peace and strive towards achieving Paradise. Muslim American Society Spokesman, Imam Warith Deen Muhammad, being interviewed on CNN Larry King live stated, "The Taliban could have been a sincere group who came to liberate the Afghan people, but the extremist views of some of their student members do not represent the purity of Islam. Islam seeks the middle path, extremist behavior and misguided deeds only serve to create confusion and hostility.

It is important that people of all religious faiths find a common ground in our common humanity. Islam unequivocally condemns the mistreatment of women, it guarantees women a full and equal position in Islam and civilized society. This is exemplified in the *Holy Qur'an* Surah 4 (Chapter) (Al Nisa) Ahyat verse 1 (The Women) which underlines the essential similarity and equal value of man and woman. O people! Be conscious of your Lord, who created you out of a single living being and created out of this mate, and from those two spread countless men and women. Without a doubt, women played a major role in the life of the Prophet of Islam (peace be upon Him) and were held in the highest esteem by him. He was liberator of the woman. Women's role in Islam and society must be one of dignity and equality. The Talibans treatment of women is un-Islamic and must be condemned by all Muslims who are guided by the righteous tenets and principles of the *Holy Qur'an* and the Sunnah (the tradition) of our beloved Prophet Muhammad (peace be upon Him). I close this brief discussion on women in Islam with Ahyat (verse 1) of Surah (chapter) 4 of the *Holy Qur'an* AI Nisa' (The Women).

> *"O mankind! reverence*
> *Your Guardian-Lord*
> *Who created you*
> *From a single Person,*
> *Created, of like nature,*
> *His mate, and from them twain*
> *Scattered (like seeds)*
> *Countless men and women-*
> *Fear Allah, through Whom*
> *Ye demand your mutual (rights),*
> *And (reverence) the wombs*
> *(That bore you): for Allah*
> *Ever watches over you."*

ISRAEL AND PALESTINE
A NEW PEACE INITIATIVE

As I am writing, I am reminded by the CNN International News that in the past twenty months of Middle East violence the death toll now stands at 1,373 Palestinians killed and 480 Israelis, this was of May 28th 2002 and still rising. I am moved to SALAAT (prayer) Surah 2 of the Holy Qur'an verse (ahyat) 153 which states "o ye who believe! Seek help with patient perseverance And Prayer: for Allah is with those who patiently persevere". The patient perseverance and prayer is not mere passivity. It is active striving in the way of Allah (God). What can be a higher reward for patience, perseverance, self-restraint and

constancy than that Allah should be with us. This promise opens
the door to every kind of spiritual wellbeing. I write not only as
a student of Islam, but also as a student of Diplomacy, International Ambassador of Peace and an Imam of Change. My passion
and compassion for building bridges of understanding, humanity
and hope and the organization of which I am the Founder and
Executive Chairman **(Global Oneness)** stand with both commitment and resolve in the fight against poverty, injustice, war,
global intolerance, hopelessness and disease.

We at Global Oneness want to empower humanity, we embrace the spirit of the human family. Specifically, we will fight
to empower the children of the world with humanity and hope
through sustainable development programs. What does this have
to do with the Middle East Crisis between Israel and Palestine.
In fact, there is a dynamic relationship? I see bloodshed of
innocent Israelis and Palestinian children everyday. These innocent children are not even given a chance to enjoy the gift of
life, much less empowerment. The perpetuators of this unending
conflict have abandoned their divine responsibility to the innocent child. I take this opportunity to personally recognize and
thank the members of the Global Oneness Family for their love,
support and encouragement in this mission. The journey of faith
continues. Encouraging a young male or female to be a suicide
bomber is both un-Muslim-like and ungodly. Our beloved Prophet
Muhammad (peace be upon Him) never encouraged any such
practice. I challenge the extremists forces in the Arab world,
that suicide bombing is not the way of the Prophet of Islam, it
is not the way forward in the search for Peace and Justice. No
matter how grave the situation is, dialogue is the only way to
reduce tensions.

If we fail to dialogue we will certainly fail in the search for
viable solutions. I support the United States Secretary of State,
Colin Powell's, view of a region where two states Israel and
Palestine will live side by side. A vision of a region where both
sides can put food on their tables and have a decent standard of
living. Both sides have to be prepared to come to the negotiating

table, and make difficult compromises. They are members of the human family. The Palestinians deserve a decent standard of living, they deserve justice and peace. The Israelis deserve the same. Justice and Peace must prevail for all. Secretary of State Colin Powell embraces and advocates the enlightened policy being pursued by the United States in the Middle East region as **"Pro Human Kind"**.

They, both Jews and Arabs, must seek the warm threshold which leads into the palace of peace and justice. In the process of gaining their rightful place, they must not be guilty of wrongful deeds. They must abandon drinking from the cup of bitterness and hatred. This is very important. You cannot bring peace to a region if there are contradictions and double standards in policy making. There must be balance and fair play.

I have always said that both sides in this conflict must have the maturity to show self-restraint. Building bridges of understanding, humanity and hope cannot be achieved in a climate of hostility and recriminations. It is never too late in the search for peace. The great writer George Bernard Shaw once said, and I quote, "Peace is so much better than war, and it is infinitely more arduous." Negotiation and compromise, as painful as they may be, are the hard choices that must be made to end the brutal cycle of terror, as is the case of Israel and Palestine. Palestine will have to make the hard choices. Israel will also have to make the hard choices. We must understand that to put an end to terrorism, you will have to first put an end to oppression. Oppression is a branch of injustice. Therefore, justice must be given to the oppressed. On the other hand, a suicide bomber will never attain lasting peace and justice. It makes more sense for both parties to engage in meaningful and productive dialogue, than to continue living in perpetual hostility. Both Israel and Palestine must recognize the fact that human life is indeed sacrosanct. Whether it is an Israeli life, or a Palestinian life, it remains sacrosanct.

We all have the same blood permeating through our veins. We have "one blood and one life" on earth. Secretary of State

Powell shares the enlightened view, so do I, that there is the potential for a region where prosperity and peace can go hand in hand, as they are both inseparable. The perpetual cycle of violence and hostility undermines any hope for a viable Peace Process to survive. There can be no world peace without universal justice and there can be no prosperity for any nation-state without Peace. Peaceful co-existence for the Israelis and the Palestinians will enhance the future prosperity of their own regions and their peoples. If the solution is a political solution, I say to both the leadership of Israel and Palestine, find the patience and courage to sit at the table of brotherhood, not necessarily forgetting past differences, but working together to understand these differences and recognize the fact that there can be a bright future where Israelis and Palestinians enjoy, what Allah (God) has ordained for them, which is the gift of a productive and meaningful life!

Without life, there can be no peace or prosperity. You must first of all have life. The United States, the only remaining super power, along with Britain, Europe and the Arab World must now focus their attention to bring a just peace to the region. Secretary of State, Colin Powell, said: "peace is not for the timid nor the tentative." It is a hard process, but a process that will ultimately save humanity.

On the day that an amicable settlement is achieved between the Palestinians and Israel, divisiveness will be erased, wars will stop, peace will be assured, and the destruction will be halted. The only hope for the area lies in convincing these two groups to live in unity as peaceful neighbors, with border security maintained between the two lands by a United Nations Peace Force. God accepts Jews, Christians and Muslims alike. All are found in Jerusalem, yet those who have faith in God, as well as those who do not have faith in God continue to fight over land, even though it only results in destruction. There have been many who have ruled the earth, but they are all gone. And there are still more to come who will rule and then pass on. No one can rule forever. Without change there can be no life. Out of darkness comes light. I was asked a question in a recent interview, "Has religion failed humanity"? My instinctive answer was yes! When we look around the world we see so much pain, poverty, suffering, wars, injustice, hopelessness, corruption, disease — all evil vices.

In the Christian world, there is suffering. In the Muslim world, there is suffering. In the Jewish world, there is suffering. In the Hindu faith, there is suffering of its people. People of all religious faiths have failed to uplift humanity. Why has religion not been able to successfully conquer all the suffering of humanity? We all say that we know God and that He is one Universal power. As religious leaders and human beings, we have however failed miserably to live in practical deeds, this universal reality.

I was once corrected by a colleague Imam, for having said, "that religion has failed humanity. I am indeed grateful for such spiritual insight, if for no other reason than that. Islam as a way of life is perfect. Allah (God) has perfected the Deen (religion) of Islam.

The Deen (religion) will not fail, but man, in his application of the righteous tenets and principles, has failed. However, the misguided application of its Divine principles by some of its leaders and followers have failed in the uplift of humanity. Their misguided deeds have brought both confusion and distortion to the pristine purity of the Islamic faith. In plain terms, many religious practitioners have perverted the truth and the divine principles which should embody sincere religious practice. That is why we have chaos and confusion in our world today. Because we have failed to understand that the lack of love amongst members of our human family, and the tendency towards domination and exploitation is the root cause of man's inhumanity to man. Let us keep it real!

Some Final Thoughts On The Middle East Crisis.

A peace conference is necessary for the region. I think it is a commendable vision of Secretary of State Colin Powell. A man of whom I have tremendous admiration and respect for, a man of strong values character and integrity, a great teacher and mentor. He is dedicated to public service and the service to humanity. He is also an International man, a Caribbean man, born of Jamaican parentage. Secretary Powell's vision is to see a region where people can live and peacefully co-exist as one human family, despite their differences. This vision, however, cannot and will not be attained unless there is mutual cooperation and mutual trust between Israel and Palestine. Secretary Powell understands the importance of a stable region to the entire world.

I humbly suggest, first to Chairman Arafat and the Palestinian leadership, that more needs to be done and a sincere effort must be made to rein in the extremist Islamic forces in Palestine who undermine any meaningful peace process. I have repeatedly stated, suicide bombings cannot and will not bring about any just peace.

I commend Crown Prince Abdullah of Saudi Arabia for his visionary and diplomatic peace initiative which gives Israel a right to exist and calls for good neighborly relations between Israeli and the Arab World. This is the way of our beloved Prophet Muhammad (peace be upon Him), a way of tolerance and mutual acceptance. Recognition of Israel's right to exist, is a step towards a positive direction that can create a climate conducive to meaningful and productive dialogue.

I also humbly suggest, to Prime Minister Sharon and the Israeli leadership that they must offer Palestinians that are disenfranchised a better quality of life. Life in a settlement under occupation is not life. If Palestinians continue to be oppressed, then hatred and dislike for the Israelis will only be intensified. President George W. Bush has asked Prime Minister Sharon, as it relates to the issue of settlements, to do what is just and right, by a withdrawal from the disputed settlements. I also share these sentiments. It is, therefore, incumbent upon Mr. Sharon to be the doer of justice. It is also incumbent upon Mr. Arafat to sincerely combat both terror and terrorism, in not only words but in practical deeds. Both leaders have not only a political duty, but a Divine obligation to their people and to the world. The madness of the brutal cycle of violence against innocent people must stop! The blame game must also stop, the killing and the hatred must stop!

The scourge of poverty, war and injustice must end for the region. Let peace, faith, love, justice and freedom ring in every village and every settlement. Let freedom ring for the Israelis and the Palestinians. Let freedom ring for the entire brotherhood of man and the sisterhood of woman. I am very passionate about this subject, because I am very passionate about the sanctity of human life, but I will close with these two sayings. The first is on the controversial subject of JIHAD (Holy War), "For man to raise his sword against man, for man to kill man, is not holy war. True holy war is to praise God and to cut away the enemies of truth within our hearts. We must cast out all that is evil within us, all that opposes God. This is the war that we must fight." The second saying comes from the Holy Qur'an, God says: "Verily Allah enjoins justice, perfection and giving help to kith and kin, and forbids all evil deeds and acts prohibited by law, as well as all kinds of oppression. He admonishes you that you may take heed".

My role as an International Ambassador of Peace representing the Universal Islamic Center of America in Jamaica and the Caribbean, and Ambassador for the Nation of Islam in Jamaica and a Imam of Change, is dedicated to the to the education of Muslims and Non-Muslims alike, as to the purity of the Deen (religion) that embodies the Islamic faith.

A MODEL FOR PEACE THE JAMAICAN EXPERIENCE

My involvement in building bridges of understanding, humanity and hope is a practical one. It is an integral part of the Global Oneness mission, which serves to embrace the human family. I may add that my formal training in International Law, International Relations and Diplomatic Practice has been very useful in this journey of faith. However, one does not have to be a career diplomat, or an Ambassador to build bridges. The foremost virtue I would say in building bridges is a fervent desire to bring humanity closer together. We live in a world beset by conflicts and tensions. We are focused on our religious differences, our ethnic differences, our tribal differences, our social and cultural differences. We have failed to acknowledge and recognize our common bond of humanity. The precious gem of freedom continues to elude us all. Freedom does not necessarily mean mere Physical or Economic Freedom, but rather a freedom that transcends geographic boundaries and most of all the freedom of our own souls. You may have money, material trappings, technological power, but that in itself does not liberate your soul from captivity. Former President, Bill Clinton, in an address to students at Harvard University stated: "There is a struggle for the soul in the 21st century". Could this soul be the soul of humanity? I would say the soul of humanity is now threatened. It is an inescapable reality that one of the greatest challenges of this generation and generations to come is the challenge to preserve the human soul, the human being.

He further went on, to advocate "that the United States in the 21st century has to spread more of its economic and political benefits." He further noted that "the United States must respect other faiths and cultures as part of the improvement of global understanding." This enlightened approach must now form a new thrust for American foreign policy around the globe. I am indeed very confident that the United States can and will lead the entire world in a new era that calls for one word, CHANGE! President Khotemi of Iran calls for dialogue amongst civilizations. This is critical in building bridges, as this dialogue, amongst civilizations cultivates mutual respect, mutual tolerance, mutual trust, mutual acceptance and makes us understand that in our diversity there is so much beauty. The tragedy of September 11th, indeed, had many positive outcomes, one of which was, that it showed America, that in its diverse cultures they are one people in one great country. America! E Pluribus Unum, "Out of Many, One."

In Jamaica, the motto is "Out of Many One People." Can and will Jamaica and America live this motto in word and in deed? One of my first official assignments in building bridges came when I was asked in my official capacity as the International Ambassador of Peace representing the Universal Islamic Center of America in Jamaica and the Caribbean as an Imam (spiritual leader, or spiritual teacher), was to use my office and connections in Jamaica, specifically in the Jewish community and in corporate Jamaica, for the purpose of reconciliation, healing and dialogue between the leader of the Nation of Islam, The Honorable Minister Louis Farrakhan on his official visit to Jamaica in March 2002.

This was no easy task. It was as a formidable one. But anyone knowing Imam Ali knows that he never backs away from challenges. My mission is to serve humanity, I have chosen Islam as my spiritual path, but my life's mission is to be of service to humanity. It was not really difficult as my earlier path to Islam was through the Nation of Islam.

I have seen the Nation of Islam grow and evolve. I have also seen the Honorable Minister Louis Farrakhan grow and evolve. I have **seen** Imam Ali grow and evolve. I was determined to build the bridges of understanding, humanity and hope between Minister Farrakhan and the Jewish community particularly in Jamaica. I was also determined to bring Minister Farrakhan in close contact with the corporate business leaders of Jamaica, who also have their own concerns about his views both recent and in the past.

I have been given the name of Bilal, by leading members of the Ministers esteemed entourage. Bilal was the African slave who Prophet Muhammad ("peace be upon Him") instructed to make the righteous call to prayer. This glorious call to prayer is referred to as the Adhan. It is the foundation of Islamic civilization.

In others words, my endeavor to get Minister Farrakhan to visit a Jewish synagogue was all part of the mission of building bridges of understanding, humanity and hope for the human family. This timely initiative was not only to advance the relationship between Christians, Muslims and Jews in Jamaica and the Caribbean, but to enhance the mission of global oneness, global tolerance, and mutual acceptance amongst all God's children on our planet earth. My initial contact in this historic endeavor was with a dear friend and brother Stephen Henriques, The Acting Spiritual Leader of the Jewish community in Jamaica. We met at a religious service at the United Stated Embassy in memory of the victims of September 11th. We have since then maintained a very close contact and friendship. Then came the process of dialogue between the Chief of Staff to the Honorable Minister Louis Farrakhan, Mr. Leonard Farrakhan Muhammad, myself and distinguished Elders of the Jewish Synagogue in Jamaica headed by the prominent Jamaican Historian Mr. Ainsley Henriques.

This process of dialogue and engagement took place at the Hilton Hotel in Kingston on Friday, March 22, 2001. It was a very honest and sincere exchange of views. It was also a valuable educational experience for us Muslims about the Jewish rituals. After the meeting at the hotel, I along with the Chief of Staff and other members of Minister Farrakhan's security detail accompanied by Mr. Ainsley Henriques and his team visited the synagogue for first hand preparation for the Saturday morning visit by the Leader of the Nation of Islam.

History was in the making and Imam Ali was about to become Bilal.

We were just a few hours away from this celebration of history and humanity which was destined to happen on the shores of Jamaican soil. I really felt like an International Ambassador of Peace as I now really understood what building bridges was all about. However, some important things had to be acquired in the next few hours. One of which, was the *Holy Qur'an*. The *Holy Qur'an* was to be presented to the leadership of the Jewish synagogue in Jamaica by Minister Louis Farrakhan. The other acquisition was much more complex. It was the acquisition of approximately one dozen Kufi's (head gear worn by Muslim men) including a very special one for Minister Farrakhan probably matching one of his elegant suits. I had to leave the hotel and go back to my home in the suburbs of Kingston and spend Friday night sorting out appropriate head gears as this is mandatory for men in the Jewish synagogue. An elegant green and white Kufi was selected for Minister Farrakhan. This Kufi was flown to me via London from Saudi Arabia as a gift a few years earlier. I thought it only befitting that the Minister should be given the best. We had to also sort out head gear for the entire entourage. In Jamaica, there are no Islamic shops. So, a simple exercise like this was a monumental task.

Then came the historic event, the departure from the Hilton Hotel in New Kingston to the Jewish Synagogue in Down Town Kingston.

Saturday morning March 23rd, 2002 at 10:00 a.m. Imam Ali, now Bilal, delivered what many initially thought was a 'mission impossible'. In a practical way, my Service to Islam and Humanity had now begun.

There was a Press Conference for about one hour after the religious service at the Jewish Synagogue where gifts were exchanged and new friendships realized.

I will now endeavor to interpret the message by the Leader of the Nation of Islam, The Honorable Minister Louis Farrakhan.

The Evolution and Maturity of Farrakhan.

"This is a message to the Brotherhood of Man and the Sister-hood of Woman. A message of Peaceful Co-existence, a New Beginning for Muslims and Jews to live together and to worship together. For nearly eighteen years, we have tried to resolve differences with the Jewish community in the United States of America. A new beginning for humanity, building bridges of Understanding, Humanity and Hope. To sit with members of the Jewish tradition, children of Abraham. My hope is that we will send a signal to the entire world. The leadership of Jamaica should applaud this bold step. If we can mend and heal the wounds between Jews and Muslims in America then ultimately, the Jews and Muslims in Palestine and the Middle East.

We must forge an alliance for progress. Building bridges of Divine Understanding. I offer you my hand in brotherhood, I offer you my hand in the resurrection of humanity to transform human life not only in the Church, Mosque, or Synagogue, but human life all over the planet earth. Pure worship for the One-ness of God. Dialogue and reconciliation, action of truth, justice and righteousness in our dealings with one another. We thank our beloved brother, the International Ambassador of Peace, Imam Douglas Owen-Ali, for his vision in making this historic visit to the synagogue a reality, may Almighty Allah bless our beloved brother Ali for his service to Islam and humanity." A member of our Jewish family called this a "Bold step of historic and epic proportions." This was indeed a United Front coming together to build in Jamaica, a Spiritual Union and to join hands in the struggle for the despised and rejected. The victory is won for the deprived of Jamaica to build a better country than we have today. Jamaica is one of the few countries in the world where Jews, Arabs and Christians live side by side in peaceful co-existence.

I cherish this positive aspect of Jamaican life. It is, however, unfortunate that politics in Jamaica and the nations political leaders never saw it as imperative to duplicate this vital virtue

92

of religious and cultural tolerance to create a climate of peaceful co-existence amongst warring political tribes.

This enlightened attitude must now be embodied in the country's national life and psyche, if we are to move forward as a productive and civilized nation. So much is, or has been, said about this issue. The challenge and the price of peace! There is both a challenge and a price for peace. It is not an "Easy Road." Can we, however, strive as not only Christians, Jews and Muslims, but as citizens of one human family, and export this new beginning of mutual acceptance and mutual understanding to the world community? Can we have a community of interests, beyond mere geographical boundaries, which will deal primarily with Quality of Life Issues? Can we move towards a Jamaica, and an America and a world where mutual acceptance is the desired goal?. Acceptance goes further than tolerance. Tolerance, however, is the beginning.

My second assignment though challenging was not as difficult. This was to organize a Private Sector luncheon in honour of Minster Farrakhan, hosted by the esteemed President of the Private Sector Organization of Jamaica (PSOJ), The Honorable Oliver Clarke O.J. (Order of Jamaica), who is also Chairman and Managing Director of The Gleaner Company Limited; the Caribbean's largest media Publication. Mr. Clarke is a notable private sector leader with considerable influence and prestige in the business community in Jamaica. Corporate Jamaica is also dominated by a considerable Jewish influence. So, building this bridge required incredible diplomacy and savvy, not only on my part, but, more so, on the part of Minster Farrakhan. The luncheon was superb, and one witnessed both the evolution and the maturity on the part of the Leader of the Nation of Islam. His wit, charm and sincerity positively affected those not only in the luncheon room at the Gleaner Company, but hundreds of anxious staff members eagerly awaiting to experience the infectious presence of the Leader of the Million Man March. The minister's passion can never change. This is a passion for the disenfranchised of the planet earth. But his evolution and maturity as a

Muslim and as a human being is to be admired. I also hosted a private dinner reception at the Hilton, Kingston where the Minister had an opportunity to engage with leading members the Jamaican society. This further provided a positive platform for building bridges of understanding, humanity and hope. Most people, get caught up in the past and fail to realize the future.

So building bridges must address old contradictions and search for new possibilities to enhance humanity. Once again, I say there can be no life without change. Minister Farrakhan's voice is a powerful one, not only in the African American community but in the entire Muslim and Arab World. It is a voice of reconciliation and healing, a voice of atonement, peace and justice. The great country of America can learn from this voice. My final challenge was to arrange a private meeting with Minister Farrakhan and a leading United States Diplomat in Jamaica at the Hilton, Kingston Hotel. The Minister once again exemplified the utmost respect, charm and sincerity in this meeting. This was another practical and momentous step in building bridges of humanity and hope. He said and I quote, "I am an American. I love my country, even although at times I may disagree with its policies. But this disagreement is not out of hate or disrespect for the leadership of the great country of America, but a burning desire to see America fulfill its great promise for humanity".

The World Champion of Peace.

Muhammad Ali took a very strong and principled position against the war in Vietnam. At that time, he was viewed by many as unpatriotic, radical an even racist. Today he is not only my personal hero, but an American and world hero. Muhammad Ali has also evolved, not only as a true Muslim, but also as a merciful and compassionate human being.

America today calls on Muhammad Ali "the greatest of all time" who "floats like a butterfly and stings like a bee" to help use his considerable influence, image and prestige in the Muslim and Arab World in the "war against terrorism." Ali (the champ) is now called upon to fight much greater battles than he did inside the ring. He now fights these battles with knock out punches of dignity and humanity. He is waging the war for the fulfillment of one humanity.

On July 10th 2002, CNN News reported Libyan Leader Moammar Gadhafi: as saying, "Libya is against terrorism." This statement is very encouraging coming from a country that has been engaged in hostility with the United States, and is opposed to United States foreign policy in the regions of the Middle East and Africa. Libya is also on the current United States terrorist watch list. This position on terrorism by the Libyan leader is a mature one and, no doubt, a step in the right direction.

My own position, therefore, on terrorism has strong support even amongst those Muslim leaders who have fundamental disagreements with America's foreign policies. The war against terrorism must maintain its focus. It has to be a Universal effort and humanitarian campaign aimed to preserve and protect innocent human lives in America and around the Globe. The mission of building bridges of humanity and hope can be achieved amongst those nations and peoples that have fundamental, social, political and cultural differences. It is all about dialogue, tolerance, respecting and honoring our differences. With dialogue, tolerance and mutual acceptance, the mission of building bridges of humanity and hope can and will be achieved. Insha Allah (God's willing).

As part of reciprocity, the mission continued beyond the visit of Minister Farrakhan. I invited members of the Jewish community in Jamaica headed by their spiritual leader Mr. Stephen Henriques and Deputy chief Mission at the United States Embassy in Kingston, Mr. Richard Smyth to a Unity Jumah (Congregational) Service hosted by the Nation of Islam in Jamaica and myself, at the Muhammad Mosque in Down Town, Kingston. The theme of the Khutbah (Sermon) was *Building Bridges of Humanity and Hope*. I called for world unity, peace, friendship and dialogue amongst all peoples and nations. I challenged the congregation to embrace a new spirit of reconciliation and healing for Jamaica and indeed the entire world. It was a small gathering of devoted brothers and sisters, but the message was profound. The media carried the positive. Once again, history was created in Jamaica, but even more important Muslims and Jews had an opportunity to acknowledge their common humanity.

I must also mention The Gulf Investment Initiative (GII) for which I am the convener. This bold initiative encourages International Investment, commerce and trade between Jamaica, the Muslim and the Arab World, specifically the Gulf-Co-operation Council States (GCC). In July of 2001, I led a team of prominent Jamaican entrepreneurs to New York to explore possible links and commercial ties between both regions. I must be very honest, there has been no dramatic foreign direct investment inflows from the wealthy Arabs states to Jamaica, as yet, for many reasons both domestic as well as international, but new possibilities have emerged from this timely initiative.

Nations that were otherwise apart, now have a glorious opportunity to come together, through investment, trade and commerce for mutual economic benefit. The seeds have been sown, the possibilities are real and we await the result of the harvest.

Building bridges requires unthinkable vision, faith and courage as there are many who are hostile to the whole notion. Because it is change and with change comes not only sacrifice, but some pain as well. The mission of building bridges of understanding, humanity and hope moves beyond the confines of tradition. We must no longer remain trapped by the confines of what we believe to be tradition. Nations and peoples are now being challenged to broaden their horizons economically, culturally, scientifically and spiritually, for humanity to become truly advanced. The Global Oneness mission of building bridges of humanity and hope embraces spirituality, humanity and commerce. We do not see these as isolated, but rather see them as having the potential for peaceful co-existence. We must empower people spiritually. We must empower people economically. We must empower people with commerce and a better economic life. We must offer humanity, paradise on earth and paradise in the hereafter. It is all inclusive. This is not only the true Islamic practice, but it is the true practice of all religious faiths. Islam embraces both the spiritual and the material advancement of humankind. "Man cannot live by bread alone. But man cannot live without bread".

Freedom, justice, equality, peace and prosperity are the liberating forces for the human family. "Freedom from Economic Depression, Justice for Every Race, Equality In Every Place."

INTERNATIONAL RELATIONS AND WORLD PEACE BUILDING BRIDGES OF HUMANITY AND HOPE. UNITED STATES CUBA RELATIONS

The United States and Cuba: A Vision for the 21st Century.

As the world staggers into the new millennium, hoping to enhance human and international relations, the prospects of a lasting and enduring world peace for the global family remains elusive. I find it both timely and relevant to briefly highlight the timeless legacy of the Madinah Charter initiated over fourteen centuries ago by the beloved Prophet Muhammad (peace be upon him). The Madinah Charter serves as a righteous and useful model as humanity continues to grapple with its own divine purpose and spiritual existence.

The Madinah Charter, written and promulgated by Prophet Muhammad for the multi-religious ten thousand-strong citizens of the city-state of Madinah in 622 A.D., is truly a remarkable political-constitutional document. The claim made by Professor

M. Hamidullah, that it was the first written constitution (FN1) in the world, is not without basis. Aristotle's Constitution of Athens (FN2), written on papyrus, discovered by an American missionary in Egypt in 1890 and published in 1891, was not a constitution. It was an account of the city-state of Athens. Other legal writings on the conduct of ancient societies have been found, but none can be described as a constitution. The Madinah Charter is the first, and, in this, it preceded the American Constitution of 1787, considered by Western authorities as "a landmark document of the Western world...the oldest written national constitution in operation" (FN3) by more than a thousand years! It also preceeded the English feudal bill of rights, the Magna Carta of 1215, by almost six centuries!

Not only is the Madinah Charter important in the sense that it is the first written constitution; it is also modern, in the sense that it was promulgated for a plural society, giving equal rights to every citizen, as well as, giving them a say in governmental matters. Considering all these, it is amazing that those Muslim leaders and writers, who talk and write about the Islamic state, seldom refer to this important seminal political document of Islam.

It is to be remembered that Muhammad had become a prophet, reciting God's revelations to his fellow-Meccans, for twelve years, before he and his followers migrated to Yathrib, two hundred and ten miles to the north of Mecca. There was going to be another ten years to his mission before he completed the delivery of the Divine message to the Arabs and to mankind in God's final scripture, the *Qur'an*. So the Madinah Charter was provisional in the sense that it could not contain all the provisions of statecraft contained in the *Qur'an*. Yathrib was later to be known as "The City of the Prophet" or simply Madinah. The reason for the migration was the growing opposition of the Quraisy aristocracy to His teachings and the receptive attitude shown by some Yathrib pilgrims at this time.

The Charter consists of 47 clauses, but due to different numbering, Prof. Hamidullah counts it to be 52(FN5). As Prof.

Hamidullah rightly stated, "...this new constitution... brought with it very important, and to Arabia at least, very revolutionary change, by providing the people with a central public institution for seeking justice, in place of everyone seeking it with the power of his own hand, or, at best, that of his family. This epoch-making innovation... brought an end, for all times, to the chaos of tribalism and laid the basis for a wider institution, viz a State." (FN7)

It should be noted that this loyalty to the State by its plural citizenry, constituted a nationalism, or more exactly a patriotism, that is approved by Islam, contrary to what some modern Muslim ideologies assert. It is in line with the teaching in the Qur'anic verse, "O people, We created you from the same male and female and rendered you into distinct peoples and tribes that you may recognize one another. The best of you in the sight of God is the most righteous." (FN8)

There were twenty districts each with a chief (naqib) and deputy chiefs (arit) and its meeting place (saqifah). The city at this time had a population of about ten thousand. Of these, the Muslims made up only a few hundred; half of it were monotheist Jews the rest being polytheists. (FN9)

It is noteworthy that the Charter ordained equality to its members and protected them against oppression. (Clause 16). The State proclaimed the brotherhood of believers and gave each one a right and support to give protection to any individual, excepting an enemy. (Clause 15). It also extended help to its members in debt or in financial difficulties in regard to payment of ransom or blood money. (Clause 12). It prohibited help or refuge to be given to a murderer. (Clause 22)

A very important human right is given in Clause 25 where freedom was guaranteed for each community to practice its own religion. The implication of this clause is that each individual was also free to choose his or her religion, in line with the clear teachings of the Qur'an. (FN10) "There shall be no compulsion in religion: the right way is now distinguished from the wrong way." (Qur'an 2:256). Note that this statement of complete religious freedom comes immediately after the grandest statement of God's power to be found in any scripture. It is indeed significant!

Another important principle of statecraft is consultation with the people in all matters. This is stated in Clause 37(a). Another important principle of just governance is that no quarter is given to injustice or wrong-doing. In the Charter, this is stated in Clause 47.

The Madinah Charter's constitution is Muhammad's **Ijtihad** (which is the fourth source of Shariah — the exercise of reason and judgement to determine the Shariah). He was confronted with the task of administering this constitution in the city state of Madinah. At this time, he had not yet received the full *Qur'an*. He had, therefore, to fall back on customs and precedents and did. In any case, all constitutions are provisional in the sense that it must be adapted to changing times.

Perhaps, in the light of present Muslim interest in an "Islamic state", we should point out that this important constitutional document of Islam does not anywhere use the term "Islamic state" or "Islamic society". The major principles governing an Islamic society are, of course, present — principles like justice, brotherhood and unity of believers, unity and cooperation among citizens of the state, freedom of religion, strict adherence to pacts entered into between parties, cooperation to do good and to prevent evil, encouragement for high moral conduct and consultation as a method of government.

It should be noted that the Charter, this first Islamic political-constitutional document, was given to the people of Madinah in the name of Muhammad, the Prophet (Clause 1), and also in the name of God as well as Prophet Muhammad. (Clause 47) Why two different ways of phrasing the ultimate source of power? It is to be remembered that during the Western Middle Ages, the Church ruled supreme in the name of God, and God's name was, of course, much misused by hypocrites and opportunists. The modern Western practice of replacing God with the people, has of course, not helped matters very much.

In the name of the people, oppression, wars, colonialism and aggressions have been launched. Thus, even in this modern age of science and technology, mankind cannot ignore a power that is greater than itself. Mankind has an autonomous right to live, and to live happily, but he must do that in a lawfully created Universe. It is in this sense that the Charter was given in the name of Muhammad the Prophet, who represented the principle of the good and right reason, which is higher than the individual person. Likewise, in Clause 47, God's name was put first, as God represents the highest Good and the highest principle of right and reason. This is necessary to conduct Man to higher and even higher achievements.

The Madinah Charter should be carefully studied by practictioners of international diplomacy. The study of this charter is also useful to conscious citizens of the global community. This visionary way of life has in its divine essence the potential for a just and equitable world.

Former President's, Jimmy Carter, official visit to Cuba in May 2002, is further evidence that the mission of building bridges of understanding, humanity and hope transcends geographical boundaries. It is an international mission that has profound implications for both the survival and the future well being of human kind. He made it very clear that he did not visit Cuba to interfere with Cuba's internal affairs. Cuba is a sovereign country, but to extend a hand of friendship to the Cuban people and to offer a vision of the future for both the United States and Cuba and for all of the Americas. The Former United States President articulated his vision that included a Cuba, fully integrated into a democratic hemisphere, part of a Free Trade area of the Americas and with our citizens travelling without restrictions and visiting each other. He expressed a fervent desire for a massive student exchange between our universities. "The people of the United States and Cuba must share more than a love of our popular music. I want us to be friends, and to respect each other." This kind of visionary initiative is what building bridges of humanity and hope is all about. It is about friendship, world unity and mutual respect through dialogue. I offer my sincere commendation to the former President for this bold and courageous effort. The dictator Fulgencio Batista was overthrown more than 43 years ago, and later the Cuban revolution aligned with the Soviet Union in the Cold War. Since then, both nations have followed different philosophical and political paths.

The hard truth is that neither the United States and Cuba have managed to cultivate a positive and beneficial relationship. The former United States President asserted; "Will this new century find us living in harmony and friendship with our neighbours? I have come here in search of an answer to this question.

He further reiterated; "Our nations have been trapped in a destructive state of belligerence for four decades, and it is time for us to change our relationship and the way we think and talk to each other. Because the United States is the most powerful Nation in the world, we should take the step toward mutual acceptance". This kind of mature discourse is what is needed if there is to be reconciliation and healing between the United States and Cuba.

As matter of fact, this is the kind of diplomatic approach required for the solution of all global conflicts. The former President echoed the hope that the United States Congress would soon act to permit unrestricted travel between the United States and Cuba, establish open trading relationships, and remove the economic embargo. Cuba can trade with more than 100 countries and buy medicine, for example, more cheaply in Mexico than in the United States. But the embargo induces anger, dislike and resentment, restricts the freedom of United States citizens and makes it difficult for us to exchange ideas and respect." He hoped that Cuba and the United States could resolve the 40 year old dispute with some creativity.

Similar problems were resolved when the former President normalized relations with China. He proposed that the United States and Cuba establish a blue-ribbon commission to add legitimate concerns on all sides, in a positive and constructive manner. He said, "Some of those who left the beautiful island of

Cuba have positively demonstrated their entrepreneurial skills. But many in South Florida remain angry over their departure and their divided families. They look to define a future so they can serve as a bridge of reconciliation between Cuba and the United States".

The Former President sincerely believes that such normal relationships are possible. He spoke of Democracy and Human Rights; not using the United States definition of "Democracy" but rather that of the Declaration of Human Rights, which Cuba signed in 1948. It is based on some simple premises: that all citizens have the right to choose their own leaders, to define their own destiny, the right to freedom of speech, to organize political parties, trade unions and non-governmental groups and to open trials. He challenged the Cuban leader, Fidel Castro, and his regime, to embrace the spirit of democratic reforms, so as to avoid being ostracized by the world community of nations.

I personally believe that the Cuban leader is very astute politically and will play his own part in building the bridges of humanity and hope for the Cuban nation and the Cuban people. Castro understands this is a new era which requires new thinking, new strategies for a country's economic, social and political survival. If you are isolated from economic progress and technological advancement, it becomes very difficult or even impossible to move a country forward. Isolation in other words induces human suffering and economic depression. This is a real fact of life. I believe at some point in time, possibly the very near future, Cuba will embrace meaningful democratic reforms, but it is my understanding that this transformation will come about incrementally. It may not be a dramatic political shift. But there will be change, as without change there can be no life.

The former President also addressed the issue of human rights. "He said, that his nation is hardly perfect in human rights. A very large number of United States citizens are incarcerated in prison, and there is little doubt that the death penalty is imposed harshly on those who are poor, black or mentally ill.

For more than a quarter century, we have struggled unsuccessfully to guarantee the basic right of universal health care for our people. Still, guaranteed civil liberties, offer every citizen an opportunity to change these laws that fundamental right is also guaranteed to Cubans. When Cubans exercise this freedom to electoral laws peacefully by a direct vote, the entire world will see that Cubans, and not foreign nations will decide the future of this country. He commended Cuba on its superb systems of health care and universal education.

Public opinion surveys show that a majority of people in the United States would want to see the economic embargo ended, normal travel between our two countries, friendship between our people, and Cuba and to be welcomed into the community of democracies in the Americas.

At the same time, most of my fellow citizens believe that the issue of economic and political freedom need to be addressed by the Cuban people. After 43 years of animosity, we hope that some day soon, you can reach across the divide that separates our two countries and say, "We are ready to join the community of democracies, and I hope that Americans will soon open our arms to you and welcome you as our friends." Former President Jimmy Carter is a true visionary, and a man of great service to humanity. Commendations are in order to this great servant of humanity. International voices like that of this human being is what is required to further enhance the Global Oneness mission of building bridges of understanding, humanity and hope for the entire human family, friendship and mutual acceptance.

The United States/Cuba relationship is a very important model for global reconciliation and healing. Animosity does not bring nations or people closer together, it only creates dislike and hostility. The time has now come, for the leadership of both these countries to engage in respectful dialogue, with the goal being that of mutual acceptance and mutual respect for each other. Former President Carter has now paved the way for this climate of dialogue and engagement. The United States is indeed a great country, and the only remaining super power, but it needs not impose its will, its values, or its economic or political leverage on a small country like Cuba. The United States must show patience and tolerance.

On the other hand, Cuba now has a glorious opportunity to liberate itself from the clutches of diplomatic, political and economic isolation. Cuba must act with practical deeds towards the political and economic emancipation of the Cuban people. The world has now radically changed, even arch-enemies today find their common bond and permanent national interests through the avenues of international trade, commerce, mutual economic advantage and technological exchange. A new era of co-operation has emerged. This new era must, however, bring Justice For Every Race, Equality In Every Place and Freedom From Economic Depression.

It is my fervent hope and belief that the United States and Cuba will embrace each other in a new spirit of friendship and mutual acceptance.

A NEW ERA OF CO-OPERATION BETWEEN THE UNITED STATES AND RUSSIA

The United States and Russia have now forged alliances. They have not only become allies in the war against terrorism, but they have also become economic and technological allies as well. Once again, this forging of alliances, is simply building bridges between both nations. Thirty years ago such an alliance between arch military and political enemies would be seen as inconceivable. But it has now happened. Both countries and their leaders have now become friends. President George W. Bush now embraces President Putin as a friend. This took great courage, and vision for this new era of co-operation to actually manifest itself.

This new era of co-operation required a new thinking and a mentality. It is incumbent for leadership around the world to embrace an enlightened philosophy that will offer humanity a genuine opportunity for freedom, justice, peace and prosperity. Russia is now a junior partner in **NATO.** After 50 years, as arch rivals and a decade of incredible uncertainty there is now a new spirit of mutual cooperation. It actually seems unbelievable. This new bond of mutual acceptance and friendship is encouraging to the mission of building bridges of understanding, humanity and hope.

The United States and Russia had the political will to sit at the negotiating table despite their obvious political, economic and cultural differences. Other nations can and must learn from this bold initiative. Ironically, on the eve of this new era of mutual co-operation, the Miss Universe Contest was won by Miss Russia. Russia has now joined the alluring world of feminine beauty and physical attraction. Nothing is wrong with that! It is actually very healthy for the male balance. But even more important, on a more serious note, the former hard-lined communist state has now embraced the doctrine of capitalist virtues, economic progress, free trade, democratic reforms and some Western values. The diversity of the Miss Universe Contest can indeed inspire a new world unity.

I sum up this new era of co-operation with an appropriate philosophy. This wise thought comes from *His Royal Highness Prince Bandar Bin Sultan Bin Abdullah Aziz, the esteemed Ambassador Extraordinary and Plenipotentiary of the Kingdom of Saudi Arabia to the United States of America. *"Commercial interests survive longer than strategic interests. When countries do business together, they stay together."* Commerce and trade has the potential and the capacity to unite peoples and countries and foster a climate of one humanity.

HRH Prince Bandar Bin Sultan Abdul Aziz
Ambassador E. and P. of the Kingdom of Saudi Arabia to the U.S.A.

*"Commercial interests survive longer than strategic interests. When countries do business together, they stay together."

*Source: A Business Guide to the Kingdom of Saudi Arabia

THE INDIA - PAKISTAN CONFLICT.

India and Pakistan are beset by conflicts over Kashmir. The United States have expressed grave concern about the possible escalation of tensions between these countries. Incidentally, the United States have requested that the sixty thousand Americans, resident in India, vacate that country with immediate effect. The United Nations has similarly requested their personnel stationed there to do the same. The conflict is now very real. The United States have stepped up the diplomatic initiative and Secretary of Defense, Donald Rumsfeld, will visit the region where he will engage in discussions with its two leaders and make the American case for self-restraint on the side of both India and Pakistan.

Both these countries are important allies of the United States in the war against terrorism. India is also a military ally of the United States, Pakistan, in particular, is a strategic partner of the United States in fighting terrorism and containing Islamic extremism. I humbly suggest that the will to continue dialogue on both sides is imperative if a nuclear disaster is to be averted. Differences must be settled at the negotiating table. Dialogue, however, is the essential component in this conflict as through it, comes the potential prevention of military hostility. We offer our sincere prayers of Divine Intervention for the innocent people of India and Pakistan May their leaders, give peace a chance! So far, the prayers of Divine intervention have been answered. The military hostility, the conflict and tension between both countries have been curtailed because of constructive dialogue. With God's help and sincere prayers, all things are indeed possible.

For my part I will continue to seek dialogue and exposure of my faith as I did at the IAAF/Coca-Cola World Junior Championships in Athletics held in Kingston at the National Stadium from July 16to 21, 2002.

Countries from around the world came to the shores of Jamaica to celebrate a memorable athletic event. This historic occasion was another milestone for Jamaica and, indeed, the global community. It was also another significant initiative in the global mission of building bridges of understanding, humanity and hope.

Commendations are in order for the organizing committee and the dedicated team that made this event possible. As the International Ambassador for peace representing the Universal Islamic Center of America in Jamaica and the Caribbean, it was appropriate to offer a hand of brotherhood and friendship to the visiting Muslim Delegation from the various countries. It was in this spirit of oneness and unity that a special Jumah prayer service was held at the Muhammad Mosque in Kingston to facilitate our Islamic family, many of whom were visiting Jamaica for the first time. In attendance, was the distinguished leader of the Kingdom of the Saudi Arabian delegation Al-Zaidi Sulaiman. The following is the text of the Khutbah (sermon) delivered on Friday, July 19th 2002:

"Today, July 19th, 2002, is a testimony that Allah tests the faithful and rewards the steadfast. Almighty Allah has brought you to the shores of the island of Jamaica to unite and bond with your Islamic family in this part of the world thousands of miles away from your homeland. This is the Divine beauty of Islam, it has no geographical boundaries, it transcends ethnic, cultural and racial origins. Allah says: 'we were made into nations and tribes, not to despise each other, but rather to get to know each other.' We are united here today in Jumah Prayer at the Muhammad Mosque in Kingston Jamaica, to begin the arduous process of unity and brotherhood as we aspire to make the goal of one United Ummah and Divine reality. We must and we will continue to make this real, beloved family. Beloved Islamic family, friends and distinguished guests, September 11th has indeed been an enormous tragedy for the positive image of Islam, but it has also provided for us, as Muslims, a glorious opportunity to show the entire world that Islam is not a religion of goatherders, paupers, fanatics, suicide bombers and terrorists. Islam is indeed the most dignified way of life that has made immense contributions to world civilization and the positive development of humanity. Islam is a religion of peace and submission to the will of Almighty Allah.

We have embraced this religious faith and way of life not by mere accident, but with the Divine permission of Almighty Allah. All praise is due to Almighty Allah for His grace and mercy. We are spiritually guided by the divine injunctions of *Holy Qur'an* and the Sunnah of our beloved Prophet Muhammad (peace be upon Him). Man can fail in his pursuits and his misguided ambitions, but the Deen of Islam can and will never fail!

I stand before you today as a baby in Islam, but a very strong baby who, Insha Allah stands prepared to do my humble part in making Islam a shining light for the people of Jamaica, and the Caribbean. Islam is indeed the most dignified way of life that has made immense contributions to world civilization and the positive development of humanity. Islam is a religion of peace and submission to the will and indeed the entire world.

Insha Allah, will give us the patience, the courage and the perseverance in this journey of Iman (Faith).

Beloved families, we ask for your hand in Divine love, unity and a new spirit of universal Islamic brotherhood and sisterhood. May this Jumah service Insha Allah, not end here with our salaat (prayers), but may it be the beginning of an enduring friendship, mutual acceptance and mutual co-operation. Insha Allah, may Almighty Allah increase us all with Divine understanding. The day is hot and the time is short so we will not hold you any longer.

Insha Allah, we will be united many times in the future. Insha Allah, we will embrace the new spirit of One united Muslim Ummah working together as one family, with one Divine Mission, the mission and the righteous cause of Al-Islam. We have many Muslim countries now visiting Jamaica for the IAAF/ Cocoa-Cola World Junior Championship in Athletics, the next time around may this visit Insha Allah, be for a World Islamic Conference. We send with you a message of freedom, justice, peace, love and unity to your respective countries and may

Almighty Allah continue to richly bless your stay in Jamaica and take you all safely back to your homes. Once again, I greet you my beloved family in peace. As Salaam Alaikum (peace be unto you)."

Recently, I note with keen interest that the White House announced it would create a permanent Office of Global Communications for the purpose of enhancing America's image around the world. At the same time, the House of Representatives approved spending $225 million on cultural and information programs abroad, mostly targeting Muslim countries, to correct what Rep. Henry Hyde, R-Ill; called a "cacophony of hate and misinformation" about the United States of America. This must be viewed as a bold initiative aimed at reducing tension, hostility and communication between America and, not only the Arab and Muslim World, but the international community.

As I have said, the way to reduce hatred and dislike is not always by the use of military, economic and technological supremacy, but the invaluable tools of dialogue, public diplomacy, negotiation and cultural understanding must also be employed to achieve the desired goal of mutual acceptance amongst peoples and nations.

Finally, there continues to be a massive escalation of hostility between Israel and Palestine. The Israeli/Palestinian conflict is now a matter of grave international concern. Innocent human beings on both sides continue to be sacrificed with no end in sight. Several initiatives have been proposed to bring about a viable political solution for both parties in this conflict.

The time has come for the world community, the United Nations, and the only remaining super power, the United States, together with the Arab and Muslim world and a global coalition to intervene in this crisis.

THE CONTINUING CONFLICT OF BUILDING BRIDGES AND THE IRAQI/UNITED STATES RELATIONS

The grave economic, political and human consequences of a war with Iraq particularly at this time would be catastrophic to the entire region of the Middle East and would impact negatively on many other areas of the world. The leadership of the United States of America should prudently utilize the options of diplomacy and international pressure, coupled with effective economical and political measures that are principled and just, in order to avert another human disaster. Military conflict should be a last resort! The value of human life must be forever sacrosanct. We pray for divine intervention as the solution to this crisis. The leadership of Iraq should allow good sense to prevail and exercise responsibility by complying to the necessary resolutions of the United Nations. The innocent Iraqi people **must not** be exposed to any further hardship and suffering. A diplomatic solution must be given every possible chance to work in this ongoing crisis. The role of diplomacy must never be underestimated in matters of human and international affairs. **Man creates war, he also has the capacity to create peace.**

Official Statement made on March 19th, 2003, regarding the imminent showdown between The United States of America and Iraq.

As Salaam Alaikum. (peace be unto you).

As a Muslim and a citizen of the United States of America, guided and committed to the righteous tenets of Islam, the Divine Injunctions of the of the Holy Qur'an and the Sunnah (traditions) of the Holy Prophet Muhammad (peace be upon Him), I humbly offer the following message.

I call for all well thinking Muslims around the world, Christians, Jews and people of all religious faiths to offer special prayers of peace, healing and reconciliation in this ongoing conflict between the United States of America and Iraq. The

111

mission of building bridges of understanding, humanity and hope between peoples and nations must now be creatively pursued if human life on all sides is to remain sacrosanct. The United States of America has been blessed with a Divine trust from Almighty Allah (God) to be the only remaining Global Super Power. Now more than any other time in world history She has to exemplify humanity and moral leadership to the world community and avoid squandering the outpouring of International Goodwill and support it received after the horrific tragedy of September 11th 2001. America now has a glorious opportunity to be a merciful and compassionate super power. Can and will She now grasp this unique moment in history?

I strongly suggest to the Iraqi regime that it should act with alacrity and offer a genuine spirit of cooperation and comply to the full unconditional disarmament demands of the United Nations. The human cost of war is catastrophic. I fervently believe that a Diplomatic miracle is still possible. "War on nations change maps. War on poverty maps change'. The price of peace is no easy goal, but it is indeed attainable. War must be a last resort!

THE CURRENT CRISIS IN IRAQ

It is now very clear that the war in Iraq is far from over. The declaration of military victory by the President of the United States of America, George W. Bush, was obviously premature. The lives of American soldiers in Iraq are now being lost on a daily basis. Yes, America's military superiority dominated the conflict and Iraq's military was simply no match against that of the United States.

However, the current reality now on the ground in Iraq is that the majority of the country's citizens celebrated the fall of the regime of Saddam Hussein. Iraqis rejoiced overwhelmingly at the demise of an oppressive and brutal system. They finally began to experience the taste of freedom.

On the other hand, the United States of America, both its political and military leadership, could have misread and miscalculated the emotional reactions by the masses as an open invitation to remain in Iraq indefinitely, and, also, that the initial military victory (by itself) would remedy the economic and social desperation of the suffering people of Iraq. As expected, it did not and will continue to be ineffective.

America now needs to clearly define both its short and long term strategies with regards to Iraq. While it will play a leading role, the initiative must not be seen as purely American. The Mission must become all-inclusive. As situations change, policies and strategies must also change and adapt to match current realities.

The reconstruction of Iraq must move from rhetoric to reality and promises be translated into deeds. The Iraqi people cannot and will not be sustained by promises of grand intentions. Their daily lives and living conditions must be attended to now!

Freedom from oppression must now be converted to economic and social freedom. Political freedom without the economic freedom cannot be sustained. America must now offer new hope to the Iraqi people and deliver on the promise of the betterment of social, political and economic conditions.

The removal of Saddam Hussein and his regime can no longer be used as bait for the Iraqis. That is the reality. The economic and social conditions of the state must be increased dramatically if America is to have any credibility, not only in Iraq and among the Islamic and Arab countries, but globally as well. Words must now be translated into deeds.

I note, with keen interest, that the congress of the United States has supported the economic initiative for the reconstruction of Iraq advanced by President George W. Bush. For democracy to be inspired in Iraq, people will have to enjoy economic and social freedom. The hatred and suspicion of America and its citizens have now escalated. This hatred is communicated not only to the people of Iraq, but also to the entire Arab and Muslim world.

I have proposed throughout this book that America's foreign policy initiatives need to be broadened and enhanced globally. It must also be balanced and consistent as a foreign policy that is contradictory leads to both hatred and mistrust.

The United States must now lead the world by example. It must endeavour to lead by inspiring mercy, compassion consideration, and justice for all. "Justice for every Race, Equality in every Place. Freedom from Economic Depression." These virtues must begin to first permeate America, and then it must be exported to the rest of the globe.

To those who continue to engender hatred through misdirected acts and deeds, I say to them, embrace the spirit of the Jamaican motto "Out of many, one people." Incidentally, the Jamaican motto is Islamic in concept. The Holy Qu'ran says, "Almighty Allah (God) made us into nations and tribes not to despise each other, but, rather, to know one another." The time has come for us to know each other, not hate each other. Out of many peoples, let us now become one nation and one world in complete unity.

I am also very pleased that the forward thinking Ambassador to Jamaica, Her Excellency Sue Cobb, has started her own mission to foster connections vis-a-vis her recent invitation of influential women in Miami, Florida to the island to begin "building bridges" of mutual economic benefit between Jamaica and Miami.

It is hoped that this will positively influence the response of the rest of the world for a New Economic Order. The goal of Global Economic Justice is attainable for the human family providing those of us, who hear and heed the voice of change, are willing to stand up and address the injustices of the world.

For this, indeed, is the intention and practice of the Spirit of Islam and the Sunnah (tradition) of our beloved Prophet Muhammad (Peace be upon him).

GLOBAL ECONOMIC JUSTICE
(A Divine World Order)

The New Economic thinking that is required is one where the bottom line becomes people rather than profit. Any approach or theory that does not speak to the global economic imbalance, but only seeks to address the war on international terrorism remains short sighted and is doomed to failure.

World Economic Injustice must now become an urgent focus of an enlightened world leadership. All nations, rich and poor, developed and developing, must move with alacrity in this matter. Global Economic Justice is the only way forward for all nations and peoples. There will be no universal peace, without universal justice.

In writing this book, it has become clear to me that restructuring the economic imbalance between the "haves" the "haves nots" and those that may never have, must be of utmost priority for the economic, social and spiritual well being of the human family. The search for a New Global Economic and Political order is imperative if human kind is to avoid continued economic, social, spiritual and moral decadence.

The solution to hunger, disease, poverty, ignorance and warfare is not an easy one. There is no magic formula. However, it is through spiritual, moral, economic and political development, that the challenges of restructuring the current global economic imbalance can and will be achieved. The great writer George Bernard Shaw once said: "Some people see things and say why, others see things and say why not." The challenges are real and the challenges are deep, but Insha Allah (God's willing) we are capable of achieving a fairer and more just world. We must now all begin to think the unthinkable! "Justice for every race, equality in every place." "Freedom from economic depression," for every citizen of planet earth. There can be a New World Economic System that offers a new hope to mankind and a system where Freedom, Justice and Equality becomes attainable for all members of the human family.

The mission of building bridges of understanding, humanity and hope is indeed a bold, courageous and timely initiative. However, this mission must convert human ideals to reality. Simply put, we must keep the mission real. For this mission to become a universal reality, there must be a global effort that will work assiduously to bring about Global Economic Justice. Until Global Economic Justice is achieved, there will be human misery all over this planet earth. All the rhetoric will not and cannot end human suffering.

Humankind is in desperate need of a Divine World Order that will move forward in achieving the goal of Global Economic Justice for the human family. Nations as well as peoples, must now see the mission of building bridges of humanity and hope as a route that can and will create a Divine World Order within the framework of Global Economic Justice. It is only therefore, appropriate that the revolutionary call for Global Economic Justice be put into perspective. I may add, with the utmost humility, that this is not some new economic philosophy. Rather, this call has been echoed time and time again. The time, however, is most appropriate and relevant, given the new global, economic, political and social realities. The positive transformation of human lives around the globe and the advancement of their well being is an enlightened view of those world citizens who dream of a better world.

The enormous tragedy of September 11, 2001, has brought home the urgent need for world economic transformation. The only remaining super power, the great United States of America must now carefully reassess and reposition its global foreign policy initiatives. The despicable and uncivilized act of September 11, 2001 has made us all realize that economic deprivation and injustice can and will lead to desperate and wicked acts by any group of human beings.

It is therefore, in this light, that I humbly call for Global Economic Justice as the only way forward for a New World Divine Order. This Divine Order is not some supernatural or idealistic position, but rather it is simply a human call for Universal Economic Justice. There will be no peace as long as Global Economic Injustice plagues our planet earth.

I say to the esteemed leadership of the United States of America with the utmost humility, the time has now come for this great nation to lead the campaign for Global Economic Justice. Like it or not, the United States of America remains the only global super power. Despite its imperfections, America is still the beacon of hope for humanity. It, therefore, has an enormous responsibility to the future well being of humankind.

There is now a glorious opportunity for the United States of America to use its prestige and supremacy around the world to advocate for Global Economic transformation. Global Economic Injustice must become a plague of the past. There must be Freedom from Economic depression. This will of course mean a visionary and dynamic outlook of American foreign policy initiatives around the world.

More needs to be done to enhance America's international image by creatively promoting its global public diplomacy efforts. This however, must be done in word and in deed. America is indeed a truly great nation. But it can become an even greater and a more respected nation globally if it pursues an enhanced foreign policy that of course will protect and preserve the vital national and security interests of the United States of America, but at the same time would work to foster a universal climate, that will promote Global Economic Justice, aimed at improving the lives of the suffering masses around the globe. If this mission is successful, or I should say when this mission is achieved, International Terrorism would be defeated, because poverty and ignorance would no longer reign predominant.

The evil terrorist would then have no space in which to operate. A desperate human being can be easily manipulated to do the most horrific acts. The war on terrorism cannot and must not be merely a military war. This is only one vital component of this global effort. The greater war that must be waged must be an economic war. This Economic war should be an International Mission led by the United States of America and its allies that will fight for this universal cause. The evil oppression that has created the scourge of Global Economic Injustice must be defeated once and for all. Let freedom, justice and liberty ring for humanity. "Justice For Every Race, Equality In Every Place, Freedom From Economic Depression."

This Divine Philosophy must be realized as we work as one human family in bringing into being a Divine World Order. This discussion would not be complete without the inclusion of the Islamic economic model as a perspective.

There are a number of Qur'anic injunctions which have encouraged Muslims to engage themselves in lawful and a wide range of trade and commerce. Some of the injunctions specially mention trade as "Fadl Allah," the bounties and excellence of Allah. There are a number Hadith of the Prophet (peace be upon Him) which also support the Qur'anic injunctions. The messenger of Allah (peace be upon Him) had engaged in trade on behalf of Lady Khadijah, and has encouraged business through is own practice. He once said: "a trustworthy and an honest and truthful businessman will rise up with the martyrs on the day of Resurrection." In yet another Hadith he has said: "a truthful, and trustworthy trader will rise up with the Prophets, the righteous and the martyrs."

The wise words of the Prophet (peace be upon Him) has given honest trading such a high status that those engaged in it are likened with the martyrs who fought and gave their lives in Jihad fisabil Allah (war in the path of Allah). An honest trader will rise up with the martyrs also means that if he continued his trade without deceiving people and without practicing usury and adhered to other principles of lawful trade, then it would be construed that he passed his life waging "Economic Jihad." How should trade and business be carried out?. The following code of conduct for Muslim traders is given in the *Holy Qu'ran*: "O you who believe, eat not each other's property by wrong means, but

---

Footnote: Since this was written the US has fought a war and occupied Iraq and the country. The President has also made requests to the congress for 800+million to rebuild Iraq.

let there be amongst you trade and business through mutual good-will." Every Muslim should live his or her life as if he or she is always in the presence of Almighty Allah (God).

We have to think that we hold all the property as a sacred trust from Allah, whether the property is in our own name or in someone else's name or belongs to the entire community. I must add, that Prophet Muhammad (peace be upon Him) made no distinction in helping the Poor and the Handicapped. He made no distinction whatsoever in these traditions between Muslims and a non-Muslims. In fact, he used to help many Jews in Madinah out of the Zakat (charity) funds which were collected by the State from only the Muslims. This is because Islam stands for the good and happiness of all mankind, Muslims and non-Muslims alike. The Muslims have been ordered to work for the uplift of all mankind and to show by their conduct that their minds and hearts are free from national or religious hatred. This is the Islam that hundreds of millions of moderate well thinking Muslims like myself embrace. It is a way of life, not of terror or hate, but of peace, justice, compassion mercy and tolerance. Hate remains and common enemy. Peace, love, justice and the embrace of one humanity should become our divine destiny. Here in lies the mercy and the compassion of this great and beloved Prophet (may peace forever be upon Him).

I am moved to tears as I study the life and the philosophy of our beloved Prophet (peace upon Him). He was indeed a mercy to the world and a blessing to humanity. I find it imperative to highlight the noble virtues of Islamic economic practice. I am by no mans advocating that all nation states adhere to this practice, simply, because all nations states are not Muslim States. However, I see the purity of the Islamic concept of trade, commerce and business activity having the potential as serving as a useful and pragmatic model in Global Economic relations. I also see it as a useful model in Individual Economic relationships as well.

One does not have to be Muslim to adhere to decent economic practice. A nation does not have to be an Islamic State to adhere to decency justice and fair play in their economic relations with other nation-states.

The Economic System in Islam as it relates to trade, commerce and all kinds of business activities if it is appropriately applied, will certainly lead to an Economic system based on fairness and equitability for all mankind. The challenge, however, is the genuine and sincere application of this model in its purity, in accordance with Qur'anic injunction and the Sunnah (traditions) of the Holy Prophet (may peace be upon Him).

A balanced attitude is the focus in Islam. Islam recognizes the importance of material well-being. To be deprived of the basics of life and to be in a state of dire poverty, is to be in a terrible state, so terrible that when the Prophet (may peace be upon Him) was asked whether the evils of deprivation equaled the evils of associating others with God, he said "yes". "Poverty", warned the Prophet (may peace be upon Him), "can lead to kufr rejection of God and ingratitude."

Beyond mainly striving to eliminate poverty, believers are urged to enjoy, and not to deny themselves the good things of this life. These are enjoyed as part of the bounty of God but should not lead to a materialistic outlook as the compelling desire to acquire more and more.

In Islam, the urge of material enjoyment is constantly tempered by the need of moderation. "O you who believe! Do not forbid the good things which God made lawful for you, and do not exceed the limits."(5:87). "Eat and drink but do not waste, for God does not love those who waste"(7:31). Such verses of the *Holy Qur'an* call for a reasonable and balanced attitude towards wealth and material wellbeing. Islam is not for life denial but for life fulfillment. In this vein, one of the most frequently-repeated supplications of the Prophet and of Muslims is: "Our Lord and Sustainer, grant us good in this world and good in the hereafter"

The complete essence of the economic system in Islam, simply put, is Individual Economic Justice, which would then lead to Global Economic Justice. Economic Justice has to begin with us as individuals. Global Economic Justice will, in my humble opinion, remain a mere "pipe dream" if some members of the human family continue to see greed, exploitation and crass materialism as some incredible virtue that makes them superior to their less fortunate brothers and sisters on this planet earth. The Great American President, the late John F. Kennedy, in his inaugural address said: "If we as a country cannot care for the many who are poor, then we will not be able to protect the few who are rich." This no doubt was a profound statement coming from a visionary and compassionate leader. The present leadership of the United States of America can reflect on such a humane philosophy. It now has a glorious opportunity to make real this profound thought from one of our greatest world leaders of this century.

There is indeed power in the word, as there is power in the mind. America can reflect such enhanced policies in its Domestic Agenda, then transcend this agenda to one that is universal both in word and deed. When this is achieved, America will become the promise for humanity. America indeed has the capability of becoming the promise for humanity and can become both an economic, military, technological and moral super power of the world. When this promise is fulfilled International Terrorism and those who perpetuate this evil would become isolated and indeed irrelevant.

I call for America to lead this campaign for Global Economic Justice not because of any bias, but rather because of the practicalities that exist. America is the only country in the world today that can significantly change or adjust world opinion or world views. If America leads the way in the mission of Global Economic Justice and a Divine World Order, then it must be a credible agenda. However, they must lead not by word, but by moral example. America would have to be a moral and exemplary voice in this initiative. As I have said, for the global mission of building bridges of understanding, humanity and hope to be successful, Global Economic Justice has to be an integral part of this purpose. For a Divine World Order to become real, human lives will have to be radically transformed. The enormous disparity between the "haves" and the "haves nots" will have to be significantly reduced.

Man cannot live by bread alone, but man cannot live without bread. I have illustrated in brief terms the Islamic economic model as a guide. I must note it is not intended to serve as some Divine solution to world poverty and economic inequality. The world is a global village made up of different groups with different religious and cultural practices. It can however, serve as a useful reminder to Muslim states and individual Muslims as to our Divine obligations. It can also serve as a useful guide to those conscious citizens of planet earth committed to decency and fair play.

In closing this segment, I have a final thought on Globalization. The principle and objective of Globalization must be to bring about economic justice and fair play amongst all nation-states, big and small alike. It must also enhance the economic status of not only the rich nations of the world, but the poor nations as well. Let us move forward with Global Economic Justice, let us make a Divine World Order Real! I humbly offer the following message for the brotherhood of man and the sisterhood of woman:

"Humankind must speak with one voice,
The human family needs a positive choice.
Destruction and decadence must no longer prevail,
The soul of man must not be for sale.
This is not the way of our Prophets,
Can't you see,
Let us all strive to build bridges
Of understanding, hope and humanity.
All this hating in the world is wrong,
Unity for Everyone,
Never again 9/11.
Freedom, Justice, Liberty,
God's way for Humanity."

Shariah: The Islamic Law by; Abdur Rahman I. Doi
ISLAM the Natural Way by; Abdul Wahid Hamid
IQTISAD The Islamic Alternative for Economics by; Bakir Al-Hassani

Conclusion

As Salaam Aliaikum (peace be unto you)

I will now focus attention on another world event that brings nations and peoples together in a manner that even the United Nations and its many diplomatic and humanitarian initiatives are unable to achieve in fostering world unity and global friendships. We refer, of course, to the wonderful pageantry of the World Cup. Many call it the greatest show on earth. The World Cup 2002, this time around, is being hosted by both South Korea and Japan. When you witnessed the proceedings of this great event, which included a grand opening ceremony of pomp and glitter, you see children in particular, in the all embracing spirit of love displaying their innocent humanity. This show of human affection on the world stage unites both peoples and nations. At the start of each game, the respective National Anthems were played and observed with mutual reverence, dignity, respect and acceptance. At the end of each game, players then exchange their shirts in a spirit of true sportsmanship and friendship. Competitive teams also show a good deal of fair play.

Fair play is an ideal that needs to transcend sports and move into the arena of human life. The diversity of nations at the world cup and the unified spirit of their many participants and players is adequate testament that there is a spark of light in human kind, just waiting to be ignited into burning flames of unity. International sporting events like the World Cup is another great forum in the global mission of building bridges of understanding, humanity and hope.

I pose this very challenging question. Can the citizens of

planet earth score the winning goals of freedom, peace, justice, liberation, from oppression and prosperity for all? The answer can only be found in the bosom of our hearts.

I now make a very fervent call to the World Islamic leadership and the Muslim Ummah (to my Non-Muslims friends and family the word Ummah in Arabic means The Universal brotherhood and sisterhood of Muslims). We must now stand up and reclaim our true Islamic culture and civilization as espoused in the tenets and righteous principles of the *Holy Qur'an* and in the Sunnah (traditions) of our beloved Prophet Muhammad (peace be upon Him).

The moderate position of the religion and the middle path which Islam encourages must be communicated to both the Muslim World as well as the Non-Muslim western world. I humbly propose and recommend that an aggressive International Public communication and educational campaign be launched as part of a new marketing initiative to expand International Islamic education.

Similarly, policy makers in the United States and the western world should embark upon an international public educational and cultural campaign aimed at articulating policy positions and the positive aspects of American and western culture. Simply speaking, there must be reciprocity and mutual acceptance. This is a vital component in the war against terrorism and its consequences.

The Islamic extremists and fanatics have successfully launched their own International Propaganda campaign of hatred and intolerance under the disguise of Islam. Moderate Muslims around the globe must now take the lead in defense of the Islamic faith. We must act now! Prophet Muhammad (peace be upon Him) believed in persuasion and education by example. The battlefield was, for him, the last resort for defending a righteous cause. But when forced into fighting for human rights, he did not flinch. That is one of the manifestations of his straight forwardness.

Another is his teachings, which established a religious practice based on respect for the basic human appetites, desires and aspirations. Although himself capable of great austerity, he did not preach asceticism to others. The Prophet being an honorable man would engage in war only for a moral or just cause. All the great battles of war that the Prophet (peace be on Him) engaged in were for an honorable, moral and just cause. The principle of righteousness was always the focus of any spiritual or worldly pursuit. He did not instruct his followers to become either revelers or renouncers. In other words, he taught healthy, honest, and responsible citizenship.

No wonder Muslims call Islam the religion of naturalness (din-i-fitrat). The revelation of the *Holy Qur'an*, with which the Prophet's personality is fully harmonious, does not put impossible demands on the will of its believers.

It reasonably leaves the question of the degree of the individual's renunciation to the individual's capacity. Nevertheless, greed and crass materialism are constantly condemned in the *Holy Qur'an*. The Oxford dictionary provides the following definition of the word "diplomacy" as applied to the conduct of international affairs. "Diplomacy is the management of international relations by negotiation, the method by which relations are adjusted and managed by ambassadors and envoys: the business or art of the diplomatist." A diplomat, then, is a negotiator "par excellence". Diplomacy, as the art of negotiation, existed before Islam. Prophet Muhammad (peace be upon Him) employed diplomacy as a means of education.

The Prophet-King of Arabia is the only King in world history who never lived in a palace, whose seat of power was practically a mud hut, and who had only one piece of furniture in his reception room for envoys: a leather-covered bolster. This he offered to his guests, contenting himself with the solid earth for his own seat. This is a Divine example of righteous, humble and exemplary leadership. Our beloved Prophet was a statesman, a humanitarian and a perfect example of a Messenger and a Servant of Almighty Allah (God). He was indeed a mercy to the world and a mercy for humanity.

The flagrant abuse and aggression of some claiming to be righteous Muslims causes great pain and concern. But leadership, however, is a sacred trust and those of us who have been bestowed with authority and position must rise up and become a new beacon of light and hope for the world to see. With the emergence of Islam on the world stage, we see the establishment of a principle which proves revolutionary for international law and diplomacy. Islam proclaims the unity of man: "O mankind! Lo we have created you from a single male and female, and we have made you nations and tribes that you may distinguish one from another. Lo! The noblest of you, in the sight of God, is the one who feareth (Him) most." Prejudices based on color, race, religion or ethnicity are absolutely condemned in Islam. Every man and woman should have an equal right to live no matter what color, class, religion or race they maybe.

We live for the day when differences between people and nations will be of no more significance than the color of the blood, which permeates all our veins. We believe that only through education that transcends certification will we as one united human family be able to temper the "Isms" that inspire human beings to be their worst enemies.

The great nation of America has a Divine obligation to pursue an "enlightened foreign policy" that is global in perspective, that will seek to protect and preserve not only the national interests of the United States and the free world, but will also foster a universal climate of enlightened tolerance, mutual acceptance, mutual friendship, peace, unity and justice for all the citizens of the world. This enlightened diplomatic initiative is an imperative strategy to combat human conflicts. America must now continue to strengthen the bonds of genuine international friendship, particularly in the Arab and Muslim world. There must be a new spirit of mutual acceptance, mutual cooperation, mutual trust and mutual understanding.

Islam provides, for the first time, the idea of a universal state based on the equality of man. In Muslim law for the first time, we came across right for the enemy at all times, in peace as much as in war, rights endorsed by the *Holy Qur'an* and the beloved Prophet. The International law of Islam seeks to regulate the conduct of a Muslim state on a just basis, not only with other Muslim states, but with the entire Non-Muslim world. This is the Islam that we should strive to embrace. This is the Islam that is now the fastest growing religion in the world today. But it is also the Islam that has been grossly misrepresented and misunderstood by many.

Our challenge, therefore, as Muslims is to bring clarity and a better understanding of our faith to the rest of the Non-Muslim world. Muslims around the world need also to be better educated about Islam. Speaking Arabic or denouncing infidels does not make one a Mo'min (believer). The positive image of Islam now has a glorious opportunity of continuing its hallmark and contributions to human civilization. We must also use the available technology to advance the cause of this great way of life.

I bring a message to the Muslim Ummah. It is not my message, as I am a mere student of Islam and a humble servant of Almighty Allah (God). Rather, I bring a Divine message from the *Holy Qur'an* (Surah 3 verse 102-103):

"O ye who believe!
Fear Allah as He should be
Feared, and die not
Except in a state Of Islam.

And hold fast,
All together by the Rope
Which Allah (stretches out
For you), and be not divided
Among yourselves;
and remember with gratitude
Allah's favour on you;
For ye were enemies
And He joined your hearts
In love, so that by his Grace,

Ye became brethren;
And ye were on the brink
Of the Pit of Fire,
And He Saved you from it.
Thus doth Allah make
His signs clear to you:
That ye may be guided."

This divine message is our freedom, this is the light for our souls, this is our eternal hope, this is our common humanity, this is our salvation. We must now rise up in oneness and submit to Divine truth and Divine knowledge. We must strive to become Mu'mins (believers).

To my Christian, Jewish, Muslim and Non-Muslim family, to my human family, I bring a Divine message, a Commentary from the *Holy Qur'an*. Introduction c. 11.

"At length came the time when the **Voice of Unity**
Should speak and declare to the People,
Without the need of Priests or Priest-craft,
Without miracles save those that happen
Now and always in the spiritual world,
Without mystery, save those mysteries
Which unfold themselves in the growing
Inner experience of man and his vision of Allah
To declare with unfaltering voice
The unity of Allah, the universal Brotherhood of man,
And the universal sisterhood of woman and grace and
mercy, Bounty and love,
Poured out in unstinted measure forever and ever."

Mother Theresa once remarked with so much compassion in her heart: "The greatest disease is the lack of love." She spoke as a devout Christian and was guided by the Divine example of the Prophet Jesus Christ (peace be upon Him) and the righteous tenets of Christianity.

I am a striving Muslim guided by the righteous tenets of Islam and the Divine injunctions of the *Holy Qur'an* and the exemplary model of Prophet Muhammad (peace be upon Him) and his Sunnah (traditions), yet we both articulate the same Divine message. This is because Christianity, Islam and Judaism though different in rituals, commands us, "Love thy neighbor as thy self. The fundamental principle and ethics of religion and religious practice in its purity ardently encourages the pursuit of ONE humanity. In a world beset by on going conflicts of war, hostility, poverty, disease, hatred and injustice we must and we will acknowledge our common humanity.

This is indeed possible, as our futures are inextricably tied to each other's action or inaction. True freedom and liberation will only be achieved for the human family only when the voices of universal unity echoes in our hearts and our souls. May Almighty Allah (God) inspire us human beings with Divine understanding and universal Love.

This short poem was written in respect of some of the many atrocities which now face the country of Jamaica and many countries throughout the entire world.

Peace and love be unto you now Jamaica!!
Our blessed land is filled with so much hate,
when the possibilities for our country are so very great.
Beloved Jamica, let us all embrace peace and love,
All this hating in me world is wrong,
Unity for everyone, peace and love must rule our land.
Imagine what a world it would be
living in freedom, justice and liberty.
Peace be unto the world!!

Surah 94 Al Sharh or Al Inshirah of the Holy Qur'an verse 1-8 (The Expansion of the Breast) is an appropriate message not only to conclude this work and discourse of ideas, but Insha Allah, I stand confident that it is a great message of inspiration that can help lift the hearts, the hopes and the aspirations of suffering humanity. This divine injunction offers real hope, spiritual and economic empowerment for humankind.

In the Name of Allah, Most Gracious, Most Merciful.

1. "Have we not Expanded thee thy breast?

2. And removed from thee
   Thy burden

3. The which did gall Thy back?-

4. And raised high the esteem
   (In which) thou (art held)?

5. So, verily,
   With every difficulty, There is relief:

6. Verily, with every difficulty, There is relief.

7. Therefore, when thou art
   Free (from thine immediate task), Still labour hard,

8. And to thy Lord
   Turn (all) thy attention".

This verse is repeated for extra emphasis. Whatever difficulties or troubles are encountered by men, Allah always provides a solution, a way out, a relief, a way to lead, to ease and happiness, if only we follow His Path and show our Faith by patience and well-doing. The solution or relief does not merely come after the Difficulty: it is provided with it. Surely with every difficulty there will come ease. I am reminded by a brother in faith and a noted Islamic scholar that the injunctions in the Holy Qur' an is the supreme power and embodies the divine solutions for all past, present and future crisis. All praise is due to Almighty Allah, The Lord of all the Worlds.

The Journey of Faith (Iman) and the international mission of building bridges of understanding, humanity and hope continues. May the human family be inspired with the true spirit of universal love. Global Oneness is indeed possible. It is in the palms of our hands. Let us now grasp it!

One love, one heart, one destiny.
Justice for every race,
Equality in every place,
Freedom from economic depression.
Freedom will endure,
Universal love is the cure.

Peace and much blessings to all world citizens.

I remain an Imam of Change and a "friend of the unbefriended poor", committed to the service of Almighty Allah (God) and to humanity. Our service to humanity, is our service to God. Insha Allah, the dream, the vision and the goal of one common humanity **must** be kept alive. I close with a message of peace and love to the entire brotherhood of man and the sisterhood of woman.

As Salaam Alaikum (peace be unto you).

Epilogue

The International Ambassador of Peace.

The date is September 11th, 2002 and we are gathered for an Inter-Faith Unity Candle Light Service to honor the memory of the victims of that horrific terrorist attack that occurred exactly one year ago. We are gathered at the United States Embassy's 'Bamboo Pen' facility in Kingston, Jamaica and the mood of is somber with some of us shedding quiet tears.

In the gathering are family members of the Jamaican victims. We all reflect on the words of Imam Ali's poetic tribute, "Voices of Unity" being presented for the first time. The words "Why? Why? Why?" haunt us as we grapple for answers.

The one thing that we are crystal clear on is the fact that the world as we knew it will never be the same. Travel, communications, commerce and cultural activities will be dramatically changed.

We, the members of the Human Family, now have to find creative ways to hold hands in unity, otherwise we will be destroyed. We will be destroyed spiritually first, and then, eventually, physically.

Brothers and sisters, let us all unite. Let us now come together and build bridges of understanding, humanity and hope.

All this hating in the world is wrong,

Unity *for* everyone,

Never again 9/11.

Freedom, Justice, Liberty,

God's way *for* Humanity.

Colin Leslie
Cultural Advisor to Ambassador Imam Douglas Owen-Ali

PRESENTATION BY

His Spiritual Eminence
AMBASSADOR IMAM DOUGLAS OWEN-ALI
at the launch of the
Global Oneness Tour
and the Gulf Investment Initiative (GII)
Conference
Ramada Hotel, New York
JULY 17- 22, 2001

BISMILLAHI ARRAHMAN ARRAHIM.
IN THE NAME OF ALLAH (GOD)
THE COMPASSIONATE, THE MERCIFUL.

Your Excellencies, Distinguished Guests, Beloved Friends, Brothers and Sisters in Islam, Members of the Diplomatic Corp, Members of the Press, I greet you with the Muslim Greeting of Peace, AS SALAAM ALAIKUM (PEACE BE UNTO YOU). I would like to record my profound thanks and gratitude to you all for taking the time out of you busy schedules this afternoon to join us in this celebration of history and humanity. I must also offer special thanks to my beloved brother in Islam Amir Abdullah Akbar and the CAPE Family for their timeless dedication and effort towards this worthy cause.

Today friends, I am deeply honored to be given the opportunity of launching two major initiatives from and for the Island of Jamaica.

THE GLOBAL ONENESS TOUR AND THE GULF INVESTMENT INITIATIVE!

We proudly record the fact these two initiatives are being launched in New York, the Center of Activity in the entire Universe. What a place to launch such Historic Initiatives! Only In New York could this happen in this way. It is gratifying to see us embracing the spirit of One Humanity. ALLAH tests the faithful and rewards the steadfast. Faith in Almighty Allah has carried us to this great city as we prepare for a Global Mission of reconciliation and reconstruction for humanity. The past has been trying and the future holds great promise. The global mission is indeed one of Faith.

First of all, I must give thanks to the Almighty Creator Allah for bringing myself and the members of the esteemed delegation safely from the shores of Jamaica in the Caribbean, to the shores of the United States of America. We are especially thankful to Our Business Leader Mr. Neville Blythe, Chairman of the UGI Group of Companies, a major private sector group in Jamaica, for his material and moral support for the mission, and all the members of the delegation, men and women of vision and purpose who are bold enough to journey here to forge new relationships, to venture into unchartered frontiers, as we search for economic and social solutions for our beloved country, Jamaica. Without these men and women this would have been another great idea waiting to happen.

I have promised myself that my presentation to you will be a brief one. I quote the saying of one of our esteemed Jamaican Patriots, "Mr. Jamaica," the late Hon. Abe Issa who once remarked: "For a speech to be immortal, it does not have to be Eternal". Some of my friends know me for being rather passionate in my speeches, but today I will defer to the wise words of the Hon. Abe Issa.

New York has always been very special for me. I owe a debt of gratitude to this very unique city as it has afforded me the opportunity for intellectual and spiritual development, and, on a more personal note, my only child, a daughter, was born in the city of New York. So you see, my beloved friends, I have many rich memories of this city. It will always have a very special place in my heart and in my life. On the humorous side, I have also had many crazy experiences here, but out of those crazy experiences came my total development as a human being and here I am this afternoon standing before you spearheading a Global Oneness Tour and The Gulf Investment Initiative.

The Global Oneness Initiative is a major humanitarian thrust for the poor and disenfranchised children of Jamaica and the Caribbean. It is our hope that we can build a better society, by investing in our children. We are seeking assistance to provide basic necessities for our disenfranchised children. Food, clothing, shelter, education and health are top priorities.

We need medical assistance for children infected with the deadly AIDS virus. We need to provide proper housing in our inner city communities.

We need to increase, dramatically, our day care centres for the children of working mothers from single-family homes in our inner-city communities. We need safe homes for our children who are abused and living on the street.

We need skills training Centres to give our young adults a life saving skill and guarantees of being able to earn an honest living as adults.

We need your help to be able to help them. Help us save our children our future generation!

Ladies and Gentlemen, Jamaica is only a speck on the map, but we are known worldwide for the great things we do as a people. Regrettably, we are also known for some negative things as well. What is certain is that we are going to be on the world stage. We have great talent, initiative, drive and spirit. We are seeking the opportunities that will make us grow and stand out as a great little nation. More and more, as we become a truly global society, we must help our bothers and sisters to reach their full potential, as, in the final analysis, we will all be better for it.

The second Initiative we are launching today is The Gulf Investment Initiative. The Gulf Investment Initiative seeks to generate US$500 million in Foreign Direct Investments for Jamaica and the Caribbean region from the Gulf Cooperation Council States, the GEC countries.

The Caribbean Region has more than one million square miles of crystalline seas, endless beaches and tropical forest. Some 40 million people live in more than three dozen nations, from the northern tip of the Bahamas to southern Guyana, from the western edge of Belize to the eastern shore of Barbados. A MAJOR RESOURCE OF THE CARRIBEAN IS ITS PEOPLE. The region has a wide diversity of cultural and historic backgrounds, with influences from all over the world blending into a rich weave of cultures and finding their expressions in the area's of music, art, dance and food.

JAMAICA, more specifically, occupies a premier position in the Caribbean. We are the third largest island and the largest English-speaking caribbean nation with almost three million inhabitants. Jamaica has received favorable ratings from multilateral financial agencies and, more recently, from Standard and Poor. The Government has had good results in so far as the macro economic indicators are concerned. Four straight years of single digit inflation? A fairly stable currency and interest rates trending downwards. We have not been as successful on the social side. It is, therefore, imperative that we increase our stock of Foreign Direct Investments.

In Jamaica, there are tremendous opportunities in the areas of Tourism? Information Technology? Film and Music? (Services generally) Agribusiness? Horticulture? Aquaculture? Light Manufacturing. Some members of our delegation would like to introduce projects, which require joint venture partners be it equity or debt financing. Financing is a major bottleneck in our country and indeed in the region.

Ladies and Gentlemen we seek to promote new commercial partnerships with our friends and family in the Persian Gulf States and the wider Muslim world. We can no longer remain trapped by the confines of tradition. The time has now come for us in Jamaica and the Caribbean region to broaden our horizons economically, culturally and spiritually, to avoid being dominated by what is termed Globalization.

The Gulf Investment Initiative seeks to define and promote

our own commercial interests as it relates to investment, commerce and trade. As a people and nations, we must venture to new heights. We can no longer afford to be guided by our traditions. Our mission is to forge and cement mutually viable commercial partnerships between the private sectors of our nations and the Gulf Region. I may also add that this commercial initiative will also include the African-American and Islamic Communities of North America.

We honestly believe that there is a great potential for investment and trade for both our regions to explore. Together, we can all make great things happen. The Gulf Investment Initiative is a milestone for our country, Jamaica, as it makes for a significant presence in the Gulf Region and the wider Muslim world; and it has come at a time when countries which were previously apart have decided to come together for mutual economic, commercial, political, cultural and diplomatic benefits.

The Gulf Investment Initiative represents a historic shift that is timely. An idea whose time has surely come! I will not rest until I see Jamaica and the Caribbean Region, a region pregnant with so many possibilities, not only in commerce, investment and trade but also with the possibility to nurture our humanity, achieve our full potential, economically and socially. The peoples of the Caribbean have fired the imaginations of all the peoples of the world. We must work toward fulfilling the Caribbean Dream.

The Caribbean must take its rightful place in the world community of nations. May God bless the Caribbean Leaders with vision. May God bless this great area of the world called the Caribbean to draw upon the reserves of its humanity and its cultural heritiage as peoples and nations and come up with the courage to excite new pathways for mutual co-operation and mutual tolerance throughout the international community.

May God bless the great country of America with the embracing spirit of humanity. May peace, justice, respect, mutual acceptance and love abound. May we strive for Global Oneness and universal friendship amongst peoples and nations. We must strive to embrace the spirit of the human family.

Dear Friends, Brothers and Sisters, I believe as nations we can fly. I am confident that together we can touch the sky. This is our moment in time. Beloved Family, I thank you and I salute you. May God bless us all.

I greet you in peace:

AS SALAAM ALAIKUM

(PEACE BE UNTO YOU)

ONE LOVE, ONE HEART

ONE DESTINY, ONE HUMANITY.

FREEDOM FROM ECONOMIC DEPRESSION,

JUSTICE FOR EVERY RACE

EQUALITY IN EVERY PLACE.

Once again, I greet you in peace,

AS SALAAM ALAIKUM (PEACE BE UNTO YOU)

Song Title: "Building Bridges"

Lyrics by Imam Douglas Owen-Ali

Introduction:

1. Bismillahi Arrahman Arrahim.
(In the name of God, The Compassionate, The Merciful).
I have been commissioned with the Divine mission of Building
Bridges of Humanity for the human family.
All this hating in the world is wrong,
Unity - For Everyone,
Never again - 9/11.
No more war,
No more hate,
It is time for us to liberate.
Freedom, Justice, Liberty,
God's way for Humanity.
As Salaam Alaikum.
(Peace be Unto You).
Shalom, Peace, Honor, Blessed.

2. All the hating in the world is wrong
Unity for Everyone
Never again 9/11. *(repeat)*

Chorus:- (repeat)
Come on Brother,
Come on Sister,
Can't you see,
We should all
Come together,
Building Bridges of Humanity.
We got to build this bridge now!

3. I have a dream that one day a world sweltering
with the heat of injustice,
A world sweltering with the heat of oppression
will be transformed
into an oasis of freedom, justice and equality.
We must make hate our enemy, and love our
universal destiny.

From the streets of Kingston,
To the streets of Harlem,
To the streets of Lagos,
To the streets of Palestine,

We can no longer sit and watch
The destruction of humankind. (repeat)

(Chorus repeat)
Come on Brother,
Come on Sister,
Can't you see,
We should all,
Come together,
Building Bridges of Humanity.

4. Muslim, Christian, Jew, the Creator made all of you,
not to hate,
not to separate, but to journey together in the
oneness of faith. *(repeat)*
Together we can conquer this global insanity with
freedom, justice and equality.
(repeat)
Our young ones all they see is war and hate,
Then they contemplate, homicide, suicide, genocide,
is what they see,
the destruction of the human family. *(repeat)*

5. Our prophets did not teach hatred and division,
it was not their way,
There must be hope for a brighter day.
We were made into nations and tribes not to despise,
not to criticize,
Not to brutalize, not to dehumanize, but to live
together as one human family, in our diversity.

No need to hate, no need to separate,
why must we, deviate? *(repeat)*

6. Let peace, faith, love and justice reign
for all,
Let us now answer a righteous call.
The people of the world don't need no weapons of mass
destruction,
What they need is global economic reconstruction.
(repeat)
Justice For Every Race,
Equality In Every Place,
Freedom from economic depression.

Salaam, Shalom, Honor, Peace, Blessed.
Come on brother, come on sister,
Can't you see,
We should all
come together.

Building bridges of humanity. *(repeat)*
We got to build this bridge now!

Copyright February, 2003

APPENDIX I

Glossary of Terms

Allah - Arabic word for the Creator.

As-Salaam Alikum - peace be unto you.

Ayat - verse of the Holy Qur'an

Deen - religion of Islam

Halal - lawful actions in Islam.

Haram - Unlawful acts or activities under Islamic law. Holy Qur'an - Holy Book from Allah, the Creator.

Imam - Spiritual teacher and congregational leader.

Iman - faith and certitude in the Creator and Islam.

Islam - A way of peaceful and righteous life for Muslims.

Jannah - Paradise.

Jihad - Self purification from ones own physical, spiritual or moral weaknesses. A Jihad of the soul is the highest challenge for a believer. (Mo'min).

Madinah Charter - Philosophy and practice of enlightened tolerance initiated by The Holy Prophet Muhammad (May Peace Be Upon Him).

Mu'min - A believer in the Deen of Islam.

Muslim - One who submits to the oneness of the Creator Almighty Allah.

Ramadan - Holy month of fasting for Muslims around the world.

Shariah - Islamic jurisprudence and injunctions from the Holy Qur'an.

Sunnah - Tradition of the Holy Prophet Muhammad (May Peace Be Upon Him).

Surah - chapter of the Holy Qur'an

Taqwah - Reverence, regard for Allah (The Creator). Ummah - The universal brotherhood and sisterhood of Muslims.

Walaikum Salaam - peace be unto you also.

Zakat - Charity.

APPENDIX II

INTERVIEW with MESSAGE MAGAZINE "JAMAICA NEEDS DIVINE JUSTICE"

Known to many as the Minister of Divine Justice and a shepherd of the less fortunate, Imam Douglas Owen-Ali is on a global mission to enhance the Islamic way of life in Jamaica, West Indies.

Imam Muhammad paid a visit to the Islamic Circle of North America's headquarters, in New York recently and spoke with **The Message**.

TM: What is your knowledge of the history of Islam in Jamaica?

Imam Ali: I am not a scholar on Islam in Jamaica, I am a student in Islam, but I know from reading that Islam is not alien to Jamaica. Many of the early slaves there were indeed Muslims. Islam came to Jamaica 600 years before Christianity, so if you were to go back in Jamaican history, you may find that the early slaves were predominantly Muslims. Unfortunately, through slavery, colonialism and then neo-colonialism, the people were taken from their roots, which was Islam.

TM: What is the overall status of Islam in Jamaica day-today?

Imam Ali: Jamaica is now ripe for Islam because of the country's overall spiritual material and moral decadence and the upsurge of materialism. Those of us in the movement of Islam believe that Jamaica is ripe for Islam. I believe for the Islamic movement, for Islam to really make a positive impact, we need to develop more strategic alliances with our global Islamic families throughout the world. We must look at ways to bring together a more organized situation. For example, right now we are at a point in Jamaica whereby if Islam is to move forward and indeed make a positive impact as we enter the 21st century, we have to not only develop strategic alliances with our global Islamic families but also tap the larger Islamic kingdoms of the world for spiritual resources (like personnel) and for material resources. This must happen if the movement is to indeed take its place in the 21st century.

TM: What is the population of Muslims in Jamaica?

Imam Ali: I would say it would be less than one percent. We have a country that is 95 percent Christians. Island-wide I would say there are 10,000 Muslims. However, this has become very fragmented because we don't have a national mosque. We have houses that are used as mosques.

TM: One of the well known Muslims from Jamaica is Jimmy Cliff. What is his role within the Muslim community in Jamaica?

Imam Ali: At present, Brother Naim Bashir (Jimmy Cliff) spends most of his time, to my knowledge in Brazil. So I would say that Jimmy has not been playing an active role in the whole Islamic movement in Jamaica.

TM: Where are you based in Jamaica?

Imam Ali: I am based in Kingston. I represent Masjid Asalaam and I am the founder of the first Millennium Islamic Centre in Jamaica. I am now spearheading an international campaign to bring the first National Mosque to Jamaica.

TM: How strong is your Muslim community?

Imam Ali: We have several small communities. Unfortunately there is a lot of fragmentation. But we would say island-wide, we have 14 parishes in Jamaica. There are seven or eight different communities; each has a following of about five hundred.

TM: Are any Jamaican government agencies assisting the Muslim community?

Imam Ali: No. Fortunately, my dream and my vision is that Islam will become a force to be reckoned with in Jamaica whereby we will have spiritual, as well as economic empowerment. The ultimate goal is for us to have a strong Muslim lobby. However, on a practical note, this will take material resources and involve having a strong economic base. If you have a strong economic base, you can influence the political direction and policy decisions of any government. But without a strong economic base, it is very difficult to influence the political direction or policy decisions.

TM: Were you in Jamaica when Dr. Abdullah Hakim Quick was based there?

Imam Ali: No. During that time I was in Africa. However, there is still a great deal of interest in Islam here since he left Jamaica.

TM: How successful has your visit to the United States been?

Imam Ali: My American tour, which will take me to New York, Washington, Atlanta and possibly Chicago, is more of a fact-finding mission. I am taking the mantle of an Ameer or International Ambassador for the Muslim community in Jamaica. Somebody has to go out there and reach the world. So, I would say, this is a fact finding mission; a networking mission to begin to build bridges with a view of going back home and sensitizing the Islamic community in Jamaica. I want to make valuable contacts with our global Muslim families, with a view of making valuable contact with particularly prominent African-American Muslims.

This is part of the whole strategy. Then the next phase will, *Insha-Allah*, involve my going on to the Middle East. That second phase of the mission will be to improve my knowledge of the Deen. I believe that Jamaica needs strong Islamic leadership and this strong Islamic leadership must come from within. We believe the leadership must be relevant to both the spiritual and material needs of the Jamaican people. *Insha' Allah*, I am hoping to go on a Middle East tour to promote my book, which is about global oneness, to improve my knowledge of the Deen of Islam and to attain both spiritual, as well as material resources for the enhancement of Islam in Jamaica, and ultimately the entire Caribbean. We see ourselves as part of an Islamic Caribbean family.

TM: Are you trying to attract the Jamaican-born Muslims in North America back to Jamaica to assist.

Imam Ali: Yes. As I said, part of the work of building strategic alliances is to build bridges and get assistance from any level. Not just economic assistance, but assistance in knowledge and personnel. It's a whole conglomeration of things to make it work. I would say that this is round one of a two-round mission.

I would like to thank the ICNA for their kind assistance. The pamphlets and other Dawah materials are greatly needed. It has come to my attention that one of the first things that we need in Jamaica is to begin to construct the Islamic Centre, a Dawah Centre where we can spread the Deen island-wide. At this time, Islam is spread with no focus, spread by word of mouth. We need a National Dawah Centre. We need to use the media, computers, and use 21st century innovations.

The Message, July 1997

▌Bibliography

Books

ABDULATI, Hammudah:
ISLAM IN FOCUS. International Islamic Federation of Student Organisations, 1990.

ADEFUYE, Ade:
CULTURE AND FOREIGN POLICY:
THE NIGERIAN EXAMPLE.
Lagos, Nigerian Institute of International Affairs, 1992.

AHMAD, Khurshid:
ISLAM: BASIC PRINCIPLES AND CHARACTERISTICS.
The Islamic Foundation.
United Kingdom—Kenya—Nigeria, 1974.

AFZAL IQBAL, Ambassador of Pakistan to Sweden and Norway.
The Prophet's Diplomacy, The Art of Negotiation as Conceived and developed by The Prophet of Islam.
Publisher, Claude Stark & Company; Cape Cod, Massachusetts 02670

'AYAD, Qadi:
FOUNDATIONS OF ISLAM.
Diwan Press, World Organisation of Islam.
DA'WA Publishing House, 1982.

CHAPRA, Muhammad Umar:
OBJECTIVES OF THE ISLAMIC ECONOMIC ORDER.
The Islamic Foundation, 1979.

DOI, Abdur Rahman I.:
SHARIAH THE ISLAMIC LAW. London, United Kingdom.
TA-HA Publishers Ltd., 1984.

ECONOMIC DEVELOPMENT IN AN ISLAMIC FRAMEWORK.
Leicester, United Kingdom.
The Islamic Foundation, 1979.

FARUQI, Ismail Al R:
HUMANISM AND THE LAW: THE CASE OF SHARI'AH.
Lagos, Nigeria. Institute of Advanced Legal Studies, 1991.

HART, Michael H.:
MUHAMMAD: THE GREATEST OF THE 100
MOST INFLUENTIAL MEN IN HISTORY
Ibadan, Nigeria. Iksam Publishers.

HAUSER, Thomas:
MUHAMMAD ALI: HIS LIFE AND TIMES.

Thomas Hauser with the cooperation of Muhammad Ali
Publisher, Simon and Schuster Inc. Copyright 1991, by Thomas Hauser and Muhammad Ali

HAYKAL Muhammad Husein:
THE LIFE OF MUHAMMAD;
Publisher, Shorouk International, 1983.

HOLLAND, Muhtar:
THE DUTIES OF BROTHERHOOD IN ISLAM.
The Islamic Foundation, 1980

HASSANI-AL, Bakir.:
IQTISAD The Islamic Alternative for Economics
Published and distributed by; IMAMIA Center P.O.; Box 275 Lanham, M.D; 20706 USA.

HAMID, Wahid Abdul.:
Islam the Natural Way
Published by; MELS - Muslim Education and Literary Services, London UK. MELS
Publishing Miami, Florida USA First Published 1989.

HOFMANN, Murad.:
Islam The Alternative (second enlarged edition)
amana Publications. Beltsville, Maryland 1418/1997.

ISLAHI, Muhammad Yusuf:
ETIQUETTES OF LIFE IN ISLAM.
Lahore, Pakistan. Islamic Publications Ltd., 1985

MUHAIY ADDEEN, BAWA M. R.
Islam and World Peace Explanations of Sufi
The Fellowship Press Philadelphia P A. Copyright 1987,
by the Bawa Muhaiyaddeen Fellowship.

A Business Guide to the Kingdom of Saudi Arabia Royal Embassy of Saudi Arabia
Commercial Office Washington, D.C. Fifth edition, July, 1996 Published by Royal
Embassy of Saudi Arabia Commercial Office Washington D.C.

MOHAMMED, W. Deen.:
Islam's Climate For Business Success.
Published by, The Sense Maker 1995 Chicago, Illinois

MOHAMMED, W. Deen
AL-ISLAM UNITY AND LEADERSHIP.
Publisher, The Sense Maker copyright 1991: W. Deen Mohammed

MOHAMMED, W. Deen:
ISLAM'S CLIMATE FOR BUSINESS SUCCESS
Publisher: The Sense Maker, 1995

MURAD, Khurram:
SHARIAH: THE WAY TO GOD.
The Islamic Foundation, 1981

NADWI, Allama Saiyid Sulaiman
Translated by AHMAD Mohiuddin.
The Life and Message of the Holy Prophet Muhammad
(peace be upon Him)
(along with a Comparative Study of Religions)
Publishers, BEGUM AISHA BA W ANY W AQF
P.O. Box No. 4178, KARACHI-2 (Pakistan)

RAHIM, A.:
ISLAMIC HISTORY.
Lagos, Nigeria. Islamic Publications Bureau, 1992

SARDAR, Ziauddin:
MUHAMMAD: ASPECTS OF HIS BIOGRAPHY.
Leicester, U.K. The Islamic Foundation, 1982

TARIQ, MaulanaAbdur-Rahman:
THE RIGHTS OF MEN.
Imran Memorial Press

The Quotable Kofi Annan Selections from speeches and statements by the
Secretary General of the United Nations.
Published by The United Nations Department of Public Information March, 1998.

Newspaper and Magazine Articles

1. *The Muslim World*, Issue #1734 March 8th, 2002 – Dhul – Hijjah 24, 1422 H.
    A weekly Published every Friday from the Muslim World League, Makkah Mukarramah.

2. *Essence Magazine*, February, 2002

3. *Time Magazine*, Special Issue, September 24th, 2001.

4. *Newsweek*, The International Magazine, February 11th, 2002.

Endnotes

1. Abdur Rahman I. Doi: Shariah, The Islamic Law, page 6.
2. Abdur Rahman I. Doi: Shariah, The Islamic Law, page 466.
3. A. Rahim: Islamic History, page 51.
4. A. Rahim: Islamic History, page 51.
5. A. Rahim: Islamic History, page 51.
6. Muhammad Husein Haykal: The Life of Muhammad, page 156.
7. Muhammad Husein Haykal: The Life of Muhammad, page 183.
8. Holy Qur'an, 4:135
9. Holy Qur'an, 5:8
10. Ade Adefuye: Culture and Foreign Policy, page 1
11. Ade Adefuye: Culture and Foreign Policy, pages 1 and 3.
12. Abdur Rahman I. Doi: Shariah, The Islamic Law.
13. Abdur Rahman I. Doi: Shariah, The Islamic Law.
14. Muhammad Umar Chapra: Objectives of the Islamic Economic Order, page 6.
15. Muhammad Umar Chapra: Objectives of the Islamic Economic Order, page 14.
16. Khurshid Ahmad: Economic Development in an Islamic Framework, page 6.
17. Khurshid Ahmad: Economic Development in an Islamic Framework, page 13.
18. Isma'il R. Al Faruqi: Humanism and the Law: The Case of Shariah, page 6.
19. Speech by the Prime Minister of Jamaica, The Rt. Hon. Percival J. Patterson.
    The Jamaica Gleaner, May 9, 1994.
20. Speech by the Prime Minister of Jamaica, The Rt. Hon. Percival J. Patterson.
    The Jamaica Gleaner, May 9, 1994.
21. Thomas Hauser: Muhammad Ali—His Life and Times, pages 514.

ABOUT THE AUTHOR

Ambassador Imam Douglas Owen-Ali, spiritual leader, author, poet, scholar, humanitarian and international relations consultant, known to many as the **"friend of the unbefriended poor"**, is a practicing and devout Muslim who adheres strictly to the Divine injunctions and the principles of the Holy Qur'an and the Sunnah (traditions) of the Holy Prophet Muhammad (SAW) (may peace be upon Him). Imam Owen-Ali attained his Masters Degree in International Law and Diplomacy from the University of Lagos, Faculty of Law in Nigeria, West Africa.

He is currently the International Islamic Ambassador of Peace representing the Universal Islamic Center of America, in Jamaica and the Caribbean and the Ambassador for the Nation of Islam in Jamaica. He is the Founder and Executive Chairman of the Global Oneness Organization, an international relations, consulting firm and humanitarian organization devoted to the upliftment of disenfranchised children in Jamaica, the Caribbean and around the world.

As the International Ambassador of Peace, Imam Ali's global mission is one of service to humanity and one of building bridges of understanding, humanity and hope for the human family. Ambassador Ali's mandate is to advance the Islamic way of life in a positive manner in Jamaica and throughout the entire Caribbean region, by espousing the enlightened concept of spiritual, moral, economic and cultural empowerment for the citizens of this region, as well as for all Citizens of planet earth.

Imam Douglas Owen-Ali has authored two other books, *Islamic Law and International Relations* and *Islamic Law and International Relations (Revised Edition)*. This, his current book **ISLAM BUILDING BRIDGES OF UNDERSTANDING. A JAMAICAN VOICE OF UNITY,** calls for a new spirit of international diplomacy, dialogue, global economic justice, a divine world order, mutual acceptance, enlightened tolerance and global unity.

Imam Ali and The Voices of Unity have also recorded a music CD on the same issue of building bridges. In terms of the CD, he explains that the song, "Building Bridges", uses hip-hop music to captivate a youthful audience with the right message at the right time, and will be supported by a "building bridges" world tour scheduled to begin in 2004. He passionately believes that with this new approach and new thinking in both the arena of human and international affairs a lasting and enduring world peace can and will be achieved for humankind.

"One world, one humanity."

www.ingramcontent.com/pod-product-compliance
Lightning Source LLC
Chambersburg PA
CBHW022018090426
42739CB00006BA/192